CERRO PALENQUE

CERRO PALENQUE

Power and Identity on the Maya Periphery

by Rosemary A. Joyce

 UNIVERSITY OF TEXAS PRESS AUSTIN

Copyright © 1991 by the University of Texas Press
All rights reserved
Printed in the United States of America

First edition, 1991

Requests for permission to reproduce material from
this work should be sent to Permissions, University
of Texas Press, Box 7819, Austin, TX 78713-7819.

∞ The paper used in this publication meets the
minimum requirements of American National
Standard for Information Sciences—Permanence of
Paper for Printed Library Materials, ANSI Z39.48-
1984.

ISBN 0-292-71140-9

Library of Congress Cataloging-in-Publication Data

Joyce, Rosemary A., 1956–
    Cerro Palenque : power and identity on the Maya
periphery / by Rosemary A. Joyce. — 1st ed.
        p.   cm.
    Includes bibliographical references and index.
    ISBN 0-292-71140-9
    1. Cerro Palenque Site (Honduras)   2. Mayas—
Antiquities.   3. Mayas—Social life and customs.
4. Social archaeology—Honduras.   I. Title.
F1435.1.C42J69   1991
972.83'11—dc20   90-21199
                                                 CIP

Dedicated to the memory of my parents,
Joanne Poth Joyce and Thomas R. Joyce

Contents

Figures

Tables

Acknowledgments

THERE ARE a great number of people whose help, advice, and criticism have been important in the development of my research in Honduras, my dissertation, and this book. Undoubtedly, I will overlook some of them, but I nonetheless would like to thank a number of specific individuals.

My research in Honduras as part of the Proyecto Arqueológico Sula of the Instituto Hondureño de Antropología y Historia was encouraged by Professor John S. Henderson of Cornell University, director of that project, and Arqueólogo Ricardo Agurcia Fasquelle, co-director of the project from 1980 and later director of the institute. I would like to thank both for giving me the opportunity to work in such a rewarding, fascinating area.

Other colleagues in PAS consistently provided stimulating conversation and welcome human contact, but I must express special appreciation to two individuals. Catherine Balfour acted as my field assistant during 1982, and without her aid far less could have been accomplished. Kevin Pope carried out his own dissertation research in parallel to mine, and I cannot express how enjoyable it was to discuss his, my, and everyone else's data with him.

My doctoral dissertation committee, consisting of Professors David Grove, Norman Whitten, Claire Farrer, and Kenn Hirth, helped me to emend the more glaring errors in the original drafts of the thesis. They of course cannot be held responsible for any flaws which remain, but they deserve considerable credit for whatever is good about the present version of my work.

Funding for my dissertation research was provided by a Fulbright-Hays Doctoral Dissertation Fellowship, an Organization of American States Trainee Fellowship, and the Graduate School, Anthropology Department, and Center for Latin American Studies at the University of Illinois, Urbana, the latter through a grant from the Tinker Foundation. Additional funding for research on collections in the United States was provided by the National Endowment for Humanities' Travel to Collections program. I would also like to acknowledge the generosity of Emeritus Professor Gordon R. Willey of Harvard University for providing funding for a research visit to Honduras in 1988, during which I undertook additional work on ceramics in the Ulua Valley.

The final debt that I owe is to my family, whose support and belief in me has been constant. Michael, Martha, Eamon, and Jeramiah Joyce provided me a place to begin writing. Tom and Linda Joyce gave me material aid at a crucial juncture. My sisters Kathy Glascott, Susan Eager, and Mary Joyce, and my brothers Brian and Tim Joyce also deserve my gratitude for their tolerance of my enthusiasm for Honduran archaeology.

Most of all, I owe the completion of the original dissertation, and of this book, to my husband and partner, Rus Sheptak. Thanks for all the tea.

CERRO PALENQUE

Chapter 1. Introduction

MY GOAL in this study of Cerro Palenque, a settlement of the pre-hispanic Ulua Valley of northwest Honduras, is to construct a context for the interpretation of the meaning of patterned material remains, in order to address a series of anthropological questions about the social organization of the people of this site. Later chapters place Cerro Palenque in the context of current knowledge of related cultures of Honduras; recapitulate the primary research that I undertook and the kinds of issues I was addressing in that research; summarize the patterning of different kinds of material remains from the site; and attempt to explicate the meanings of these patterns, drawing upon general anthropological theory. First, the terms under which I have operated in my research, and operate in writing this book, must be briefly considered.

Archaeology as Anthropology

In North America, archaeology has traditionally been included as a major branch of anthropology, a situation not inherent in the discipline, as comparison with the inclusion of European archaeology in history makes clear (Trigger 1978:1–36; Willey and Sabloff 1974; Hodder 1986:9–11). If archaeology is anthropology, what kind of anthropology is it? And how does archaeology differ from ethnology, the other major branch of anthropology?

The most obvious difference between archaeology and ethnology is in the kinds of evidence they study. Archaeology draws on material remains to understand human experience and cultural process (Deetz 1988:17–18). Archaeology contrasts with ethnography and historiography, which depend respectively on behavior and documents for their interpretations (ibid.:13, 16–18). The kinds of issues which archaeologists or ethnographers study are a separate issue: archaeology is distinguished first and foremost by its dependence on observations about the material record, rather than direct observations of behavior.

Practitioners of archaeology, ethnography, and historiography construct written accounts of human experience, process, or culture (Deetz 1988:16). In each case, the account is about a past state of affairs, a past which may vary in scale (ibid.: 15–17). The constructed accounts represent "projected contemporary thought about past actuality integrated and synthesized into contexts in terms of culture, sequential time, and contemporary values and interests" (Deetz 1988:15, following Taylor 1948:34–35). James Deetz (1988:18) suggests that if ethnography is what cultural anthropologists do, then what archaeologists do could be called "archaeography," "the writing of contexts from the material culture of past actuality." Both ethnography and archaeography provide cases for the comparative science of ethnology (ibid.:20).

Archaeological research, then, embodies two distinct phases. The first is the production, through analysis of material remains, of observations about a past actuality, organized partly by contemporary thought about the past. The second is the construction of written accounts of past actuality, drawing on these observations. Both steps are essentially interpretive.

Archaeology as Interpretation

Given the definitions proposed, archaeology can be considered a methodologically distinct form of anthropology. Archaeology differs in taking as its object of study, not the behavior of people, but the material remains which they leave behind. Just as ethnographies stem from diverse anthropological points of view, so archaeographies may reflect different concerns.

The model of anthropology I adopt in this study begins with the assumption that the object of ethnography is to construct a written account based on observations of behavior, which articulates culturally specific symbolism, to interpret culture, which is a web of meanings within which people act (Geertz 1973). What cultural anthropologists do is ethnography, a process of "thick description" (ibid.:6–7). The object of ethnography, in this model, is to outline a hierarchy of meaningful structures, determining their social grounding and import (ibid.:7–9).

Since the ethnographer begins with, and systematizes, observations which are themselves interpretations, ethnographies are interpretations. Their subject is behavior, which is symbolic action or the articulation of culture. Culture, a web of meanings, is itself a context within which social events, behaviors, institutions or processes can be intelligibly described. The test of the validity of an ethnographic interpretation, a constructed reading, is its coherence (Geertz 1973:5–17).

Archaeographies, or archaeological ethnographies, have the same status as interpretations as other ethnographies. They are dependent on observations of material patterning, rather than behavior, but their ultimate concern is the same: the coherent, intelligible explication of the articulation of culture, conceived of as the constructed meanings specific to a particular place and time.

This model of archaeological practice has recently been characterized as a "symbolic realist approach to social theory" (Lamberg-Karlovsky 1989:11–12), beginning with the premise that all knowledge is symbolic construction, each construction based on a particular model of articulation. C. C. Lamberg-Karlovsky (1989:11) warns against using this fact as a justification for "uncritical relativism in which all perspectives are equally good," but endorses pluralism, which "does simultaneously recognize the significance of difference and particularity in the comparative study of social process. Commonality and difference are held in tension: an indispensable aspect of dialogue. Dialogue becomes the instrument for the creation of relationships, not for the achievement of a uniformitarian understanding of cultural evolution." This dialogue is achieved, I would suggest, through the process of writing archaeological texts and the reading of such texts by others.

On Writing the Past

Anthropological writing has been a topic of intense concern to contemporary ethnographers (Clifford 1988; Clifford and Marcus 1986). A "focus on text making and rhetoric serves to highlight the constructed, artificial nature of cultural accounts . . . The notion that literary procedures pervade any work of cultural representation is a recent idea" (Clifford 1986:2–4).

In an examination of how contemporary archaeological reports use rhetoric, Ian Hodder (1989) identified a shift toward impersonal and objective style, away from the personal, sequential accounts of the late eighteenth century. I would suggest that this is accounted for primarily by the image of archaeology as a "natural science of society" (Lamberg-Karlovsky 1989:10, citing George E. Marcus and Michael M. J. Fischer [1986]). Hodder (1989:271–272) identifies specific characteristics of the modern field report which are explicable as devices of the natural sciences, including the replacement of sequential narrative by archaeological typologies and the elimination of any account of the development of particular interpretations.

These shifts are part of the more general promotion of ethnographic writing to the status of science, in which "the facts of the matter may be kept separate, at least in principle, from their means of communication," and "literary language" is "scientifically condemned for lacking 'univocity'; the purportedly unambiguous accounting of natural science and professional history" (Clifford 1986 : 4–5). The final report presents categories of remains, reducing the mass of observations (themselves first-order interpretations) to a purportedly objective description of facts. It eliminates all that is particular and personal in the interpretation in order to project the impression that the conclusions reached are natural and inevitable. "The authority of the text is to be placed outside the self in the faceless, objective discipline" (Hodder 1989 : 273).

The question of authority has been central to contemporary concerns about ethnographic writing. "How is unruly experience transformed into an authoritative written account?" (Clifford 1988 : 25). Ethnographic writing involves taking an experience and translating it into a text, and a text which is concerned not merely with interpretation but with authority. In the pluralistic debate engendered by interpretation, the relative merit of different accounts becomes a topic of concern. Experiential authority is often used as a solution for the prospect of uncritical relativism (Clifford 1988 : 22). I believe the appeal to experiential authority offers only the illusion of a solution and is an invitation to diversion of debate from the content of particular interpretations to the personality of particular interpretants.

I suggest that the assertion of authority itself must be renounced in favor of the pluralism Lamberg-Karlovsky celebrates (1989 : 11–16). The fact that the knowledge constructed by archaeologists is "inherently *partial*—committed and incomplete . . . need not lead to ethnographic self-absorption, or to the conclusion that it is impossible to know anything certain about other people" (Clifford 1986 : 7). Nor does this realization rule out the construction of "truthful, realistic accounts" (ibid. : 25). I would suggest that particular interpretations of the past will be judged as they traditionally have been: by the readers who adopt, ignore, or refute them through their application to different cases or newly generated observations, verifying in the traditional fashion the truthfulness and realism of those accounts.

In this book, I adopt a nontraditional style and organization self-consciously. Like the early archaeological reports Hodder (1989) discusses, in this book I attempt to make clear the progress of research and interpretation as a sequence during which both goals and ideas changed. I highlight the historical contingency of my interpretations. Following Lamberg-Karlovsky's observation that "the reciprocity which should exist between analysis and narrative must enjoin a particular point of view" (1989:13), I first clarify several topics crucial to the interpretation embodied in the chapters which follow.

Archaeology and Meaning

Ethnographies are based on observations of patterns of interaction between people. Crucial are verbal interactions, including acts as simple as naming and as complex as the production of metaphoric speech. That part of the ethnography of living cultures which is based on patterns of words is largely inaccessible to archaeology. However, patterns of objects also figure in the construction of the webs of meaning which bind people together. These patterns may be as simple, and basic, as the layout and features of a house or palace (Geertz 1980) or as complex as the iconography of a public monument (Schele and Miller 1986). The archaeological ethnography is, consequently, based on patterns of objects. These patterns, established by the behavior of the vanished members of past societies, were meaningfully constituted and provide the grounding of archaeological interpretation.

The process of archaeological interpretation begins with the definition of contexts, by identifying those aspects of the data which relate to the meaning of a particular item, given a particular question or concern (Hodder 1986:139). Archaeological interpretation, like ethnographic interpretation, requires the selection of significant variation. As in ethnography, this selection derives its support from the coherence of distinct dimensions of variation, made mutually intelligible by the proposed interpretation (Hodder 1986:135–136).

A distinction may be drawn between two distinct types of meaning that are explicated archaeologically: the meaning which the archaeologist infers from the relationships between archaeological remains (for example, the association of specific types of ornaments with males and others with females, based on burials) and the culturally specific meaning which is the content of symbols (Hodder 1986:121–122). While any archaeological ethnography necessarily deals in the first type of meaning, fewer touch on the specific content of symbols. The majority of this study is concerned with the identification of contexts for the explication of systemic meaning, inferred from the relationships (similarities and differences) between archaeological remains.

Archaeological interpretations depend on the kinds of patterns perceived and the questions asked of the particular case. The first question that must be answered in order to begin the construction of this archaeological ethnography, then, is "What do I want to understand about the people of the precolumbian site of Cerro Palenque?"

Anthropological Issues of Interest

Three basic anthropological questions underlie my attempt to understand Cerro Palenque. How are people organized in groups? How do these groups interact with similar and different groups? How do these groups of people and their interactions change through time? At the end of the third chapter, I restate these questions specifically with respect to Cerro Palenque, after providing the background necessary for the reader to understand these more specific questions. At this point, the three questions are general propositions common to many anthropologists. They are distinguished by their concern with people as members of groups.

Anthropology is concerned with processes and structures which are significant beyond the level of the individual. This level, on which groups are defined by shared culture, is usually referred to as *society* (Firth 1963:27–28). The three questions share an emphasis on the social realm, but they are differentiated by the polarity between social statics and dynamics.

The enduring skeleton of society is usually conceived of as *social structure*, patterns or rules which govern the behavior of individuals within the society (Firth 1963:28–33). Kinship, economy, and polity are all included in social structure, depending for their continuance not solely on the individual but on the survival of the group as a whole.

The interpretation of social structure, the statics of society, has presented particular problems for the archaeologist. Without direct testimony from the vanished population, the nature of the family, the order of political structure, and the kind of economy rest on inference from material remains. Archaeologists have tended to simplify complex issues and to assume causal linkages between different parts of social structure. Typological assignments of archaeological societies, in which the nature of some institutions is implied by the inferred presence of others, have been the result.

Social dynamics, on the other hand, has been one of the specialities of archaeologists. Social dynamics includes interaction (synchronic dynamics) and cultural evolution (diachronic dynamics). Archaeologists have been comfortable with the inference of change through time, because they can directly contrast the patterns of remains at different points in time. Archaeologists find the presence of foreign objects plain evidence of interaction. It is interesting that it is the *processes* which are represented by these evidences of social dynamics—in other words, the kind of social structures which they represent—that are controversial. Everyone may agree that a particular site grew radically in size; but some may find this convincing evidence of the emergence of a new political form, while others dispute this inference.

In attempting to interpret the patterned material remains from Cerro Palenque as evidence for particular social structures and social dynamics, I will necessarily be making inferences. In this, the study of this site resembles not only all other archaeological works, but also all ethnographies. Anthropology, whether the anthropology of living peoples based on their verbal testimony and behavior or the anthropology of vanished peoples based on their patterned material remains, is an interpretive endeavor.

Inference and Ethnographic Analogy

The interpretations advanced in any archaeological study are likely to be based on analogy with ethnographically observed cases. The validity of this procedure must be assumed, since it cannot be directly demonstrated. Archaeological investigations of sites formed by the activities of living groups whose behavior was observed may seem to promise such demonstration. In fact, such ethnoarchaeological studies cannot be given privileged status, since an argument for their utility in explaining past behavior must rest in the first place on an assumed analogic relationship with the past case. Unlike some archaeologists, I do not believe the assumption that ethnographic analogies can be used is either more or less problematic than any other assumption of comparability in anthropology. Ethnographic analogies may be preferable to other sources of interpretation, such as unconstrained imagination, in that they describe the way some human beings at some specified place and time have behaved.

Archaeologists can try to specify how and why particular analogies will be drawn. Traditionally, decisions about the use of analogies have been based either on assumptions of direct historical continuity from the past to the present (Steward 1942) or on theoretical frameworks such as cultural ecology (Price 1974). A theoretical approach will dictate greater attention to certain factors given greater weight by the theory, providing a means to select appropriate analogies. The cultural ecological model suggests that analogies should be drawn between societies exploiting similar environments in similar ways (Price 1974:452). The analogies derived will be general, cross-cutting linguistic and cultural organization.

The use of specific, historically grounded analogies based on the assumption of direct historical continuity is more common for the Maya area (Vogt 1964). Beginning with the assumption of a conservative cultural core or structural armature, direct historical analogies try to account for the variation introduced by historical distance in order to base explanations of past behavior on better-documented examples. Thus, Evon Z. Vogt's (1969) detailed data on settlement patterns in the contemporary Highland Maya community of Zinacantan have been applied to the archaeological record of the Classic Period Lowland Maya (Bullard 1964; Vogt 1964). As Barbara J. Price (1974:448–449) notes, the directness of continuity from Late Classic Tikal to modern Zinacantan is not necessarily clear. Perhaps more problematic is the necessary assumption that the unique historical circumstances of the intervening centuries, notably including the Spanish Conquest, Colonial Period, and post-revolutionary period, had no significant impact on the characteristics under study. Recent studies of the post-hispanic historical processes affecting Guatemala and Honduras resoundingly document adaptation across the native societies of these countries (Adams 1989; Watanabe 1990).

In later chapters, I make use of the Maya settlement data from Zinacantan as a comparison for Cerro Palenque. I do so despite assuming a lack of direct historical continuity between these two sites. I employ the data from Zinacantan as an almost uniquely well documented general analogy. I base my use of Maya data, and data from other Mesoamerican cultures, on the apparent comparability of environmental, social, and ideological context, embodied in the characterization of these cultures as "Mesoamerican." The formation of Mesoamerica (including the Ulua Valley during the period of occupation of Cerro Palenque) resulted in shared historical development which lends greater weight to comparisons of unrelated Mesoamerican societies. Within Mesoamerica, the selection of general analogies (both archaeological and ethnographic) rests on the theoretical perspectives I adopt.

Theory and Interpretation

The interpretation detailed in the chapters which follow draws on three specific theoretical strands. The first is an explicit model of social dynamics emphasizing the way social power is developed and exercised (Adams 1975). The second is a theory about relationships between political power, knowledge, and geographic distance particularly apropos in an area usually described as the frontier of Mesoamerica (Helms 1979; 1988). Finally, I draw on regional economic theory which attempts to explain some aspects of settlement pattern in terms of economic relations (C. A. Smith 1976), while reinterpreting these observations in light of substantivist critiques of formal economic models.

The central concept of social power is defined as a relationship based on perceptions of differential control over an object or goal (Adams 1975:9–20). Power is the ability to influence the behavior of others because of their perception of your control over an object or goal, regardless of the validity of this perception or the basis of the perceived control (ibid.: 106–121). The formation of relationships of power, through hierarchical centralization, contrasts with the development of coordination between parties with perceived common interests (ibid.: 208–217).

This model focuses attention on the formation of perceptions of differential control, an essentially ideological process. Mary W. Helms (1979; 1988) presents detailed discussions of the formation of such perceptions in precolumbian Panama and across a wide spectrum of cultures. The common feature of the cases she describes is the presence of a cosmology which equates distance in space with distance from the natural world (Helms 1988:20–65). Those with access to spatially removed areas can employ the knowledge of these areas as a path to authority (ibid.: 131–171). Since only some members of society are able to travel, they can claim differential control of whatever good is ascribed to the distant. By using material goods from distant areas, travelers can create the perception of greater control which is the basis of social power.

Relationships between Honduran societies and those of the Maya Lowlands seem to have been used in the fashion suggested, as a source of material goods which signaled a distinctive access to distant areas. Throughout Mesoamerica and Lower Central America, distance in space seems to have been equated with distance from the natural world; so these claims are also claims to privileged access to the supernatural world.

The movement of material goods from Mesoamerican societies into Honduran societies was apparently politically motivated in its inception. Because of the association of these goods with the distant, they reinforced the formation of relations of social power. However, the economic relations formed also had long-term material consequences for the Honduran societies. Dendritic networks of politically motivated economic integration (C. A. Smith 1976) created the potential for competition between Honduran societies. Reorganization of political and economic systems in the Maya Lowlands was able to affect the organization and development of Honduran societies. The emergence and decline of Cerro Palenque as the preeminent settlement in the Terminal Classic Ulua Valley can be understood in light of these developments.

Chapter 2. Archaeological Background

CERRO PALENQUE is an archaeological site in the Ulua Valley of the northwest coast of Honduras, Central America (Figure 1). An exception to the extremely mountainous terrain of most of Honduras, the Ulua Valley is a broad, long alluvial valley formed by three major, and numerous minor, rivers (Figure 2). The largest is the Ulua, which enters the valley from a narrow gorge on the southwest, and turns north toward the Caribbean about 15 kilometers east, at the hill named Cerro Palenque. At this same point, the Ulua receives its major tributary, the Comayagua, which enters the valley from a similar steep gorge on the southeast. Augmented by the smaller Río Blanco, the Ulua and Comayagua form a major tropical river which winds sinuously 120 km to the sea. At the time that the site of Cerro Palenque was a living community, this river was joined 25 km north by the third major river, the Chamelecon, which drained the Naco, Quimistan, and Sula valleys to the west (Pope 1985 : 66). Today the Chamelecon occupies an abandoned channel of the Ulua and makes its way separately to the sea.

The river system in the Ulua Valley is the major force influencing the form of the land. The rivers follow a tropical seasonal pattern, falling to a low during the dry season from November through March and swelling with the rains which begin in April or May. Although controlled for the most part today, in precolumbian times the annual rise of the river culminated in the overflow of its banks and flooding of the lower, flat plains on either side. The heavy load of nutrient-rich sediments was dropped on the river banks, building fertile river levees up above the level of the valley floor. Water which had overflowed these banks was trapped in the lower area on either side, forming water-logged backswamps. Beyond the reach of the flood-waters on the east and west were the first terraces of the mountains, cut by smaller streams. In the Ulua Valley, the west side of the valley also included a series of low, open hills which interrupted the back-

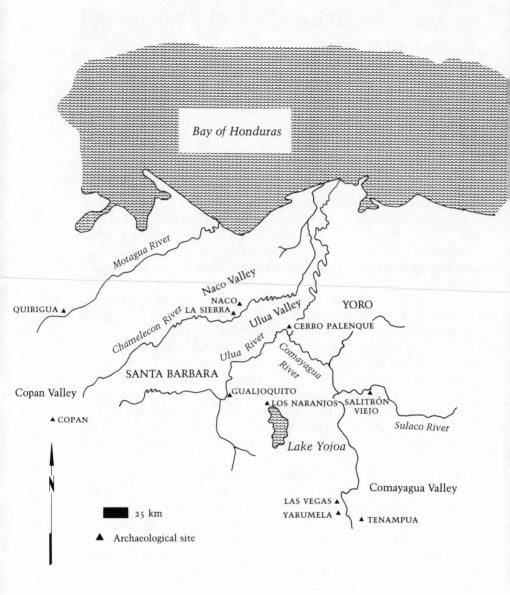

Figure 1. Honduras: major areas mentioned in text.

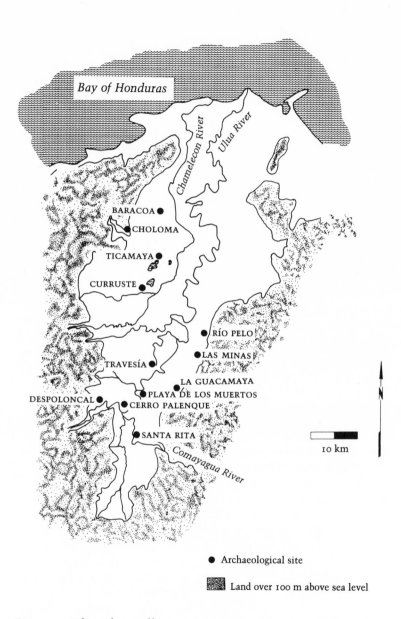

● Archaeological site

▨ Land over 100 m above sea level

Figure 2. The Ulua Valley: major sites.

swamps. Cerro Palenque is the southernmost peak of one of these sets of hills.

The agricultural potential of the different geographic features— river levees, backswamps, and uplands—was quite variable. In a study of a similar river system on the Mexican Gulf Coast (Coe and Diehl 1980) river levee lands were considered potentially more productive than uplands. Levees yielded more per unit area than uplands (ibid.:80), and although uplands could be planted twice per year, levees could be continuously cropped without resting (ibid.:69–72).

Backswamps, left unmodified, are unsuitable for agriculture (cf. Coe and Diehl 1980:34, 69, 143), but elsewhere they were the site of the most productive means of agricultural modification practiced in the Americas. By excavating trenches and using the excavated earth to build up adjacent areas, it was possible to construct systems of canals and fields raised above water level (Denevan 1982). These raised-field systems created a network of arable, well-watered land and canals offering abundant water-life. Periodic mucking out of the canals onto the fields enriched the soil with organic nutrients. At present, there is no evidence to indicate the use of raised-field systems in the Ulua Valley, but naturally abandoned river levee segments in the central valley, a site of intense occupation around AD 700, had a similar potential (Pope 1985:159–171).

The natural resources available vary greatly within the valley. A recent study summarizes the plants and animals which would have been available (Pope 1984). Deer, monkeys, tapirs, and peccaries were the largest land mammals, and all were potential sources of food. Birds include the predators, hawks and eagles; various parrots, which would have been valued for their colorful feathers; and the edible turkeys, curassows, ducks, and other marsh birds. The rivers would have provided caimans, turtles, small crabs, fish, and shellfish, while the proximity of the ocean meant the potential availability of marine fish and shellfish as well. A variety of native fruits, the avocado, sapote, nance, and others, and palm seeds including the coyol and corozo were available as well.

Geological resources were also varied. The Ulua Valley cuts through at least four distinct kinds of rock formations (Elvir 1974; Williams and McBirney 1969). In the far south, flows of vesicular lava are exposed over wide areas (Williams and McBirney 1969:21– 27, 63–64, 70–72). The southeastern valley edge and a tiny area on the southwestern valley edge are formed by volcanic rhyolite tuff (ibid.:31–45), welded ash in thick layers which is easily worked into blocks and sculpture. Along the majority of the southwestern valley edge and forming the backbone of the Cerro Palenque hills were formations of alternating limestone and cobble conglomerate layers (ibid.: 14–17). The cobbles, derived from a variety of earlier rocks, included quartzites and cherts, material suitable for use as chipped stone tools.

A major geologic fault south of the Chamelecon River divides the rocks of the southern valley from much older, igneous formations which bound the northern valley (Elvir 1974). These include granites, diorites, and metamorphosed sedimentary rocks: schists, gneisses, and marble (Williams and McBirney 1969: 5). Because the Chamelecon drained these formations, which were high in the mineral mica, the clays of the Chamelecon and of the Ulua below its confluence with the Chamelecon were mica-rich. Clays from the northern and southern valley, and the ceramics formed from them, can be distinguished by the presence of this shiny mineral.

The people who lived on the riverbanks had direct access to few of these lithic resources, except on the Comayagua where massive cobble beaches were formed. People closer to the various resources had available some but not all of these materials. Yet rhyolite blocks were used at archaeological sites on the Ulua River, vesicular lava was employed throughout the valley for corn-grinding tools, and more exotic materials (marble, schist, cherts) were found far from their natural sources. The nature of the processes of interaction which spread these materials throughout the valley will be one topic of this study.

The People of the Ulua Valley

Archaeologists do not have living informants to tell them what the language and culture of the people they study were like. Written texts sometimes identify the language, and culture is usually re-defined by archaeologists as material culture, the tools, ceramics, houses, sculpture, and other manufactured objects whose remains are recovered archaeologically. The traditional means for adding flesh to the bones of material remains are the use of ethnohistoric accounts of western contact with indigenous cultures and ethnographic analogy from surviving descendants.

For the Ulua Valley, the use of either of these sources of information is limited. No indigenous culture survived to be documented by modern ethnography in the Ulua Valley. Equally persuasive arguments have been offered for using what little is known about each of the indigenous cultures of Honduras, the Paya, Jicaque, Lenca, and Chorti, in order to interpret the prehistory of the Ulua Valley. The Ulua Valley offers no texts which would directly settle the point, and seems to have been in a zone of intense interaction between the cultures of Honduras. A beginning point in addressing this question would be the identification of the earliest recorded information pertaining to the Ulua Valley.

Hernando Cortés marched to Honduras in 1523 to quell a rebellion on the northeast Honduran coast (Chamberlain 1953). His overland route took him as far as the Naco Valley, west of the Ulua plain, where he was told about other towns in Honduras. One of these, "Tholoma," is almost certainly Choloma in the northwest Ulua Valley. Cortés went from Naco to the seacoast, apparently without entering the Ulua Valley. The first detailed commentary on the people of the Ulua comes from Andrés de Cereceda, the first governor of the colony of Santa María de Buena Esperanza, located in the Sula Valley west of Naco.

Santa María was settled in an area where the indigenous population had already cooperated with Cortés. Like many Spanish colonies, it quickly ran into problems because the settlers were soldiers, not farmers. Relations with the local populace became strained, and Cereceda lost authority. Onto this stage came the first named indigenous figure from the Ulua Valley, the *cacique* Cisumba. He encouraged the people of the Sula Valley to rebel against the Spanish colony, and the rebellion led to a mutiny by the colonists against Cereceda. Demanding to abandon the colony and move to the more viable Spanish town of Trujillo, on the northeast coast, they forced Cereceda to flee. While he was on the road east to Naco, a settlement still friendly to the Spanish, the mutiny was quelled by the opportune arrival of Pedro de Alvarado, sometime conqueror of Mexico City and governor of Guatemala.

Alvarado had been drawn to Honduras through a complex interchange involving Fernando de Montejo, governor of Yucatan, who had been assigned as the new governor of Honduras (Sheptak 1987b). For various reasons Montejo delayed his departure for Honduras and, in a disputatious correspondence with Alvarado, seemed to cede the governorship to him. Alvarado immediately set off to rescue the beleaguered colony and establish a firm claim. His arrival convinced the colonists to return to Santa María, while Alvarado himself carried the battle to the source of the trouble, with Cisumba in the Ulua Valley.

Alvarado was successful in his military campaign, despite Cisumba's efforts to build palisades on his riverside base and notwithstanding the aid of reinforcements from the Maya lord of Campeche under the command of Gonzalo de Guerrero. Guerrero, a Spaniard who chose to ally himself with the Maya, was killed on the battlefield, and Cisumba was defeated. The documents which Alvarado issued immediately thereafter, establishing the city of San Pedro de Puerto de Caballos and dividing the region among his supporters, provide the most detailed information available on the prehispanic population of the Ulua Valley. (The following discussion is based on Sheptak 1983; see also Lara Pinto 1982; Wonderley 1984a.)

Alvarado lists towns in the Ulua Valley, some of which can be identified with modern locations along the major rivers. He describes the settlement of Cisumba, at Ticamaya, as the chief of the river and tallies the strength of this town and its major subsidiaries. Unfortunately, he gives us little information directly related to the language and culture of the people in the Ulua. We know that they had established ties to Yucatan, not only because of the reinforcements sent by Yucatec Maya lords, but also by the incidence of place names along the river which are apparently Yucatec. These names are often paired with others in a pattern which suggests double naming and consequently the use of two languages, but the identity of the second language is uncertain.

Possible candidates are diverse. East along the coast were the Paya, Chibchan-speaking, and inland were the Jicaque, speaking a language of Mesoamerican affiliation (Campbell 1976; 1979). South, and probably west, were Lenca-speaking groups (Chapman 1978 : 16–22). Lenca, a language with no known relatives, has features transitional between Mesoamerican and South American languages (Campbell 1976). It has two major subgroups, Salvadoran and Honduran Lenca, both extinct today. Other languages, such as Nahuatl and Chorti or other Cholan Maya, have also been suggested as the language of northwestern Honduras.

For a variety of reasons, I have argued that the language of this area was a dialect of Lenca, with a long history of contact with Cholan, specifically Chorti, as a high-status language, and a less extensive history of contact with Nahuatl-influenced Yucatec as a language of status (Joyce 1988a). I believe "Toquegua," a language recorded for the northern Motagua Valley just west of the northern Honduran coast (Feldman 1975) is a comparable example. Lists of Toquegua personal names include some which are Cholan, some which are Nahuatl, and a majority uninterpretable as either. Toquegua itself may be identifiable as a Lenca word. Place names ending in the syllable "gua" are found throughout the area of Lenca speech in central and southern Honduras and El Salvador, where linguists believe Lenca has been spoken for millennia. This place-name pattern extends to towns in the Naco, Sula, and Motagua river valleys. In addition, the Lenca place name "Quelepa," "Place of the Jaguar," is re-

corded for central Honduras, for El Salvador, and, in 1525, in the
northern Motagua Valley (Andrews V 1976; Stone 1957; Sheptak
1983:11).

If Lenca extended to the Toquegua area of the Motagua Valley, it
is likely that adjacent northwestern Honduras was also Lenca in
speech. Some support for this position can be gleaned from meager
ethnohistoric sources. A Lenca ceremony called *guancasco* was recorded for towns in the Department of Santa Barbara south of the
Naco Valley and west of the Ulua Valley (Adams 1957; Titulo de
Yamala n.d.). One such ceremonial included the town of Ilama, politically part of the Naco Valley, whose name is Nahuat. The use of
Nahuat calendrical personal names recorded for the Naco Valley
(Lara Pinto 1982) follows a pattern noted as a prestige practice by
J. Eric S. Thompson (1970:8–31) for the Chontal Maya of the Usu-
macinta drainage, in which only the day name, and not the numer-
ical coefficient, was used.

The possible identification of the people of the Ulua Valley as
Lenca makes available only a very little ethnographic information
(Chapman 1978; 1985; Castegnaro 1989; Adams 1957; Stone 1948).
Anne Chapman (1978:36–37; 1985:84–86), on cultural grounds,
and Lyle Campbell (1976; 1979), on linguistic grounds, identify the
Lenca as a Mesoamerican people. The linguistic definition of Mesoamerica identifies an area of intense linguistic interaction leading to
shared vocabulary, syntax, and figures of speech (Campbell 1979).
Lenca is included in the Mesoamerican linguistic area, although it
shows evidence of being on its periphery. Lenca was influenced
linguistically by Cholan speakers, Classic Lowland Maya, including the Chorti of the western Honduran site of Copan (Campbell
1976). It also was influenced by the Jicaque language and the non-
Mesoamerican Paya language (Holt and Bright 1976). Perhaps most
significantly, Lenca is one of the many languages that have Mixe-
Zoquean loan words that appear to be derived from the earliest
Mesoamerican civilization, that of the Olmec of the Mexican Gulf
Coast in the first millennium BC (Campbell and Kaufman 1976). The
Lenca word for cacao, like its counterpart in many other Meso-
american languages, was a Mixe-Zoque loan word.

Mesoamerica, geographically the region including most of Mexico, all of Guatemala and Belize, and part of Honduras and El Salvador, was originally defined as a culture area marked by practices
shared by speakers of particular languages (Kirchhoff 1952). Mesoamerican peoples were agricultural, with maize and beans occupying a primary place; they also grew and used other crops, such as

chile, avocado, and cacao. Certain religious beliefs and practices, including a ritual calendar with periodic festivals, were also common to Mesoamerican peoples. These aspects of Mesoamerican cultural identity were shared by the Lenca. Lenca were agriculturalists, growing corn and processing it by soaking in lime and hand-grinding (Chapman 1978 : 30–31).

Very little reliable information is available on the political and social makeup of Lenca communities (Chapman 1978 : 23–27). The direct testimony of ethnohistoric documents suggests the existence of some chiefs coordinating some areas, as in the case of Cisumba's authority over the northern Ulua Valley (Lara Pinto 1982). In contemporary Lenca towns (Chapman 1985 : 21–22), households consist of a thatched-roof house of one or two rooms, with storage in the rafters. The second room may be specialized for use as a kitchen, with hearths on the floor or a raised table. These households always include a small altar consisting of small images placed on a table, which is decorated for ritual with wild flowers and plants. In traditional communities, production of ceramics takes place within the household, as a specialization of women (Castegnaro 1989).

Reportedly, the sixteenth-century Lenca used a Mesoamerican-style 365-day calendar with 18 months of 20 days and observed ceremonies marking each month (Chapman 1978 : 35–36). Scattered information from the sixteenth century (Chapman 1978) and contemporary oral tradition and ritual (Chapman 1985 : 98–107; Stone 1948) provide indications that Lenca cosmology shared basic Mesoamerican concepts of the structure of the universe and the place of human beings within it. Modern Lenca conceive of the world as composed of two planes, the heavens and the earth, each composed of seven layers. Lenca altars, conceived of as the center of the natural world, are oriented east, the direction of the rising sun. The four cardinal directions form the four corners of the natural world. During ritual, a dual division between right and left is maintained, with the left, southern side, associated with the earth, and the right, northern side, associated with the heavens. The ritual specialists are associated with the heavens, the person for whom the ritual is conducted with the earth. Shrines mark the location of supernatural spirits who inhabit wells and the summits of mountains (Chapman 1985; Stone 1948).

Belief in a supernatural animal double is part of the Lenca world view (Chapman 1978 : 32–33; 1985 : 211–214). The most powerful of these *naguales* is the feline. The survival of the animal double is essential for the survival of the human being. Perhaps related to belief in *naguales* is a tradition, recorded in Spanish sources, about a mythical woman named Comicagual, or "Flying Jaguar" (Chapman 1978:33–34). This woman was credited with arrival from a foreign place of origin to the central settlement of her time. Skilled in magic, she transported through the air a stone idol, which gave her victory in battle. Eventually she turned over political control to her three sons, born without a father, sometimes described as her brothers. These men became the ancestors of later Lenca rulers. Comicagual herself disappeared in a flash of lightning, turned into a beautiful bird which ascended to heaven.

The story of a founding magical female of distant origin who turned over rulership to three brothers, perhaps her sons, recalls similar founding mythology in Classic Maya texts at Palenque (Lounsbury 1985) and the Postclassic Quiche Maya *Popol Vuh* (Tedlock 1985).

Contemporary Lenca ritual is centered on ceremonies addressed to the spirits, held in the house, fields, or other appropriate location (Chapman 1985). These rituals take place at important points in the maize agricultural cycle, at the initiation of activities such as pottery making, and at points in the life cycle. Ritual specialists, together with their wives, run these ceremonies, for themselves or for others. Prayers, burning of incense, and the offering of cacao beans and sacrificed birds to the spirits culminate in a meal of cacao drink, maize beer (*chicha*), chicken, turkey, and tamales. The cacao and chicken are consumed only by the ritual specialists and their wives, while maize beer and turkey are eaten by other participants. The chicken, a foreign bird, is sacrificed to the spirits of the heights, while the turkey's blood is offered to the earth spirits through a hole in the ground.

Zomos, wild epiphytic bromeliad plants of the genus *Tillandsia*, are an integral part of the altars for rituals. Stemming from the highest trees of the mountain forests, they are the vehicle to transfer offerings to the mountain spirits. Orchids can substitute for these plants. Cacao beans are an important component of offerings to spirits during ritual. Copal, a tree resin, is offered as incense in ceramic burners. Both copal and cacao are said to originate outside the natural world in the four cardinal directions.

Shamanism, for curing and divination, is also practiced by contemporary Lenca (Chapman 1985:197–209). Tobacco cigars are used to identify the cause of illness. Divination is also practiced through the reading of grains of corn and seeds of cacao.

Contrasting with these domestic rituals is the Lenca ceremony of *guancasco*, which involves reciprocal visiting by delegations that carry with them the image of their patron saint (Chapman 1978 : 30; Stone 1948; Adams 1957). Masked dances and speeches emphasizing peaceful relations between the communities are part of the *guancasco*. The precolumbian ceremony may have counteracted the lack of centralized authority to settle disputes between communities, disputes which could have been sparked by the control of scarce arable land.

These scattered pieces of information suggest that the Lenca were hierarchically organized, with ceremonies and cosmological traditions related to those of other Mesoamerican societies. I assume that the precolumbian inhabitants of the Ulua Valley were Lenca speakers. The identification of the Lenca as Mesoamerican justifies greater reliance on general analogies with other Mesoamerican peoples, including the Maya. However, more important is the demonstrable Mesoamerican character of archaeological remains in Honduras, reviewed in the next section. Regardless of the languages they spoke, the precolumbian peoples of Honduras during the heyday of Cerro Palenque were part of the greater Mesoamerican world.

Honduran Archaeology: Time Periods and Cultural Stages

Archaeologists generally make use of two kinds of concepts to organize their results: time periods and cultural stages. Often, unfortunately, these are confused, a confusion particularly encouraged by the practice in Mesoamerica of naming time periods with stage names. Cultural stages refer to a level of development, either implicit or explicit. For example, a particular culture might be defined as "Classic," meaning that it had achieved its highest level of cultural elaboration; or as "Decadent," meaning that it was on the decline from a peak of development. These designations are stages, and as such need not imply contemporaneity.

Far more common than the use of stages is an organizational framework of more or less arbitrary time periods. The beginning and ending dates for time periods in American archaeology are usually set by the development of some phenomenon which is considered to take place at the same time across wide areas (a "horizon style"), or else is made equivalent to some cultural development at a single place (Willey 1945; Willey and Phillips 1958 : 29–34).

Archaeology in Honduras began in the nineteenth century (Stephens 1969; Maudslay 1889–1902; Gordon 1896; 1898a; 1898b; 1902; Squier 1853; 1870). Major contributions to the definition of chronology were made throughout the first half of the twentieth century (Popenoe 1934; Vaillant 1934; Strong, Kidder, and Paul 1938; Stone 1941; 1957; Canby 1949; 1951; Epstein 1957; 1959). Syntheses of the archaeology of Honduras have appeared at regular intervals (Strong 1948; Glass 1966; Healy 1984). These have presented chronological reviews, at first employing the general Mesoamerican framework of Preclassic (or Formative) (900 BC–AD 250), Classic (AD 250–800) and Postclassic (AD 800–1520) time periods. The transition dates in this system were set to coincide with the absolute dates (derived largely from the Maya calendrical inscriptions) of events in the Maya Lowlands. More recently (Healy 1984), an alternative temporal framework has been employed for Honduran archaeology, with numbered periods beginning with a paleoindian Period I (to 8000 BC), and following with Period II (8000–4000 BC), III (4000–1000 BC), IV (1000 BC–AD 500), V (AD 500–1000) and VI (AD 1000–1550). Period IV is further subdivided into early and late (IVa: 1000–300 BC; IVb: 300 BC–AD 500).

The transition dates for several of these periods differ markedly from those of the Mesoamerican periods and reflect instead local, perhaps Central American, changes in material culture, especially ceramics, a revision first suggested by Claude Baudez (1966). Recent archaeological research in Honduras has tended to confirm the utility of the alternative system of periods, while refining both the dates of transition and the nature of changes apparent through time. As a consequence, Cerro Palenque and the Ulua Valley can be placed in context in Honduran prehistory.

Period IVa: The Middle Formative

With the exception of scattered preceramic remains, the Middle Formative is the earliest period for which secure archaeological information exists throughout most of Honduras. Five regions are of particular interest at this time: the Copan Valley; Yarumela, Comayagua; Los Naranjos, on Lake Yojoa; Playa de los Muertos and related sites in the Ulua Valley; and the caves of Cuyamel, on the northeast coast. These sites span the entire period from ca. 900 BC to ca. 200 BC, with both early and later Middle Formative remains.

Early Middle Formative, ca. 900–600 BC, is represented by remains from Copan, Los Naranjos, Yarumela, and probably the caves of Cuyamel. At Copan and Cuyamel, ceramics from burials exhibit incised designs clearly related to those of the Olmec symbol system of Mexico (Fash 1985; Gordon 1898a; Healy 1974). The use of caves as burial sites in both areas is complemented in the Copan Valley by deeply buried remains of early houses along the river (Fash 1985 : 136–140), including subfloor burials also accompanied by incised ceramics and elaborate jade ornaments.

The early Middle Formative ceramics from Honduras are particularly evocative of those from Central Mexican Highland sites such as Tlatilco (Porter 1953). They share the use of bottle forms and particular abstract motifs derived from the caiman and the shark (Joyce et al. 1986). These ceramics in Highland Central Mexico are evidence of participation in interaction networks with the Gulf Coast Olmec culture (Grove 1981; Coe 1965; Flannery 1968). Participation in the same sphere of interaction may be indicated by the Honduran ceramics. Linguistic evidence supports this idea. Mixe-Zoque loan words in Honduran languages including Lenca, especially the word for cacao, have been interpreted as evidence of contact with the Gulf Coast Olmec civilization (Campbell and Kaufman 1976). At this early date, routes of exchange of cacao, and perhaps other goods such as jade from the Motagua Valley, extended into Honduras (see Healy 1974).

While early Middle Formative ceramics were associated only with modest house remains in the Copan Valley, and were found only in burial caves in northeast Honduras, at Los Naranjos on Lake Yojoa the first large, earthen structure was constructed at this time. This development seems to be part of a more general pattern typifying contemporary southern Mesoamerica, including the site of Yarumela (Canby 1949; Joesink-Mandeville 1987) and the El Trapiche group of Chalchuapa, El Salvador (Sharer 1978). At each of these sites, a single very large structure was erected and later renovated as part of a large, loosely organized plaza group formed by lower, but still impressive structures.

Yarumela and Los Naranjos contrast in basic ceramic inventory at this time period (Canby 1949; 1951; Joesink-Mandeville 1987; Baudez and Becquelin 1973). This regionalization of Period IV Honduran ceramic complexes extends also to Copan (Viel 1983) and to the Playa de los Muertos culture of the Ulua Valley (Popenoe 1934; Vaillant 1934; Strong, Kidder, and Paul 1938; Agurcia 1978; Kennedy 1978; 1980; 1981; 1982b), although all of these sites share an emphasis on monochrome pottery and decoration by plastic techniques, including incision, zoned burnishing, appliqué, and modeling. Only the rare burial ceramics seem closely comparable across the area.

Participation in wider Mesoamerican interaction networks may continue during the later Middle Formative (ca. 600–200 BC). A cache of greenstone celts at Los Naranjos has been interpreted by the excavators (Baudez and Becquelin 1973) as evidence of contact with, and influence from, the site of La Venta on the Olmec Gulf Coast. Such caches of celts, also found at contemporary Chiapa de Corzo, Mexico (Lowe 1981:242–252), and Seibal, Guatemala (Willey 1977:138), appear to be another feature of Formative Period culture which spread through the interaction network. The contemporary ceramic complex at Playa de los Muertos lacks the elaborate incised decoration noted in early Middle Formative burials elsewhere in Honduras, and instead shares the Mesoamerica-wide adoption of the simple "double-line-break" motif on bowl rims (Kennedy 1978; 1980; 1981; 1982b).

Period IVb: The Late Formative and Early Classic

The development of Honduran ceramic complexes during Period IVb, the Late Formative through Early Classic, stands in marked contrast to the regional diversity of Period IVa. Surface treatment, forms, and decorative motifs associated with the Usulutan tradition spread throughout Honduras and El Salvador (Demarest and Sharer 1982; 1986; Demarest 1986; Sharer 1978). Usulutan ceramics emphasize painted decoration (in multiple-line resist patterns) instead of plastic decoration and introduce an emphasis on orange as a background color which persists in Honduras throughout the Classic Period. Ceramic complexes from the Copan Valley (Viel 1983), Naco (Urban 1986a:77–79; Urban and Schortman 1988), Santa Barbara (Schortman, Urban and Ashmore 1983:29–30), the Ulua Valley (Joyce 1985:65–90, 476–522; Robinson 1987:159–177; 1988:13–20, Wonderley 1988), Lake Yojoa (Baudez and Becquelin 1973), Comayagua (Canby 1949; 1951; Joesink-Mandeville 1987), and the Sulaco Valley (Hirth 1988:302–310; Kennedy 1982a) all participate in this new development.

While most known Period IVb sites are buried beneath later sites, destroyed to form fill for later constructions, or destroyed by natural processes, such as erosion by rivers, a few have preserved architecture. These include Santo Domingo, Naco (Henderson et al. 1979; Urban 1986a; 1986b), Yarumela, Los Naranjos, and sites such as Río Pelo (Wonderley and Caputi 1983) and La Guacamaya (Robinson 1982; 1987) in the Ulua Valley. While at Yarumela and Los Naranjos this occupation continues that of the preceding period, at Santo Domingo, La Guacamaya, and Río Pelo, the new sites are first founded in this period. They continue the use of earthen construction, loose plazas, and tall structures typical of the preceding period.

Late in Period IVb, throughout the well-studied regions of Santa Barbara, the Sulaco Valley, and the Ulua Valley, as well as in Copan, ceramics decorated in trichrome, and rarely in polychrome, on an orange background begin to make their appearance. While these developments are significant, as they presage the dominance of Period V polychromes, they are numerically less important than the development of bichrome ceramics, in which red paint is added to the orange slip and Usulutan resist ceramics. Red-on-orange bichrome ceramics are diagnostic of the Early Classic equivalent late Period IVb in the Ulua Valley, the Sulaco Valley, and Santa Barbara, and are present at Copan, in El Salvador, and on the northeast coast of Honduras. Late Period IVb also seems to be the time during which many, if not most, Period V sites were first established. At the same time, some existing sites were abandoned, their buildings left intact until much later reoccupation or squatter use. Because most sites established in later Period IVb continued in use in Period V, it is almost impossible to say anything about the nature of settlements and their extent at this time. This is the time that the first known settlements were established on the northeast Honduran coast (Healy 1978b). At Copan, the first Maya inscriptions and monuments date to this period, while the development of ceramics was strongly influenced by developments in the Guatemala Highlands (Riese and Baudez 1983; Viel 1983).

Period V: The Late Classic

Period V, the Late Classic or Polychrome Period, appears to have been the peak of settlement throughout Honduras. Copan grew to its greatest size, the majority of its monuments were carved, and it evolved a unique local ceramic style, Copador Polychrome (Fash 1983b; 1986a; Beaudry 1984; Viel 1983). Settlement in the Copan Valley was at its most elaborate, with the greatest diversity of sites (based on size and architectural features) and greatest number of sites. In all of these features, Copan is typical of developments in Honduras during this period, when regional, distinctive polychrome ceramics flourished and the greatest number and diversity of sites developed.

At least three levels of settlement are found in most areas (Hirth et al. 1981; Hasemann 1985; 1987; Agurcia 1980; 1986; Dixon 1987; 1989; Joyce and Sheptak 1983; Robinson 1982; 1986; Urban 1986a; 1986b). These include at least two levels with sites that have architecture which, by its size, elaboration, and materials, appears to reflect high labor investment and may have public functions. In the Ulua (Stone 1941; Joyce 1982; 1985), Naco (Strong, Kidder, and Paul 1938; Henderson et al. 1979; Urban 1986a; 1986b), and Comayagua valleys (Stone 1957; Agurcia 1980; 1986; Dixon 1987; 1989), at Lake

Yojoa (Baudez and Becquelin 1973), and in Santa Barbara (Ashmore 1987), some sites with public architecture from this period include identifiable ballcourts. Ballcourts are specialized facilities indicating participation in the spread of the Mesoamerican ballgame.

It is probably not coincidental that these are also the regions where polychrome ceramics related to Copan's Gualpopa and Copador traditions, or to the Ulua Polychrome tradition of the Ulua-Yojoa-Comayagua corridor, are found. These ceramics are those which strongly suggest Classic Maya polychrome traditions of the Lowlands and Highlands of Guatemala and Mexico. The corridor defined by the Ulua Valley, Lake Yojoa, and Comayagua is the area which has been the focus of research as the Maya frontier (Lothrop 1939; J. E. S. Thompson 1970; Longyear 1947; Henderson 1978), and the Naco Valley and Santa Barbara would be included within the interaction sphere of the Maya of Copan by most researchers (Henderson et al. 1979; Urban and Schortman 1988; Schortman et al. 1986).

East of this corridor, only the Sulaco drainage and the northeast coast have received significant archaeological attention. The Sulaco drainage manifests a three-level settlement system (Hasemann 1985; Hirth et al. 1981). This area was the center of development of a series of ceramics including a unique polychrome style, the Sulaco Polychrome (formerly Bold Geometric), which was much imitated in the areas immediately to the west and apparently was traded to the Ulua Valley (Kennedy 1982a; Joyce 1985; Hirth 1988:314; personal communications, 1986–1988). Sulaco polychromes appear to have close relations to the San Marcos Bold Geometric polychromes of Selin Period Northeast Honduras (Epstein 1957:133–138, 154–155; Healy 1978b:62, Fig. 7b; Strong 1948:80, 143, Fig. 4).

Recent survey along the Cuyumapa River in Yoro, north of the Sulaco Valley, located comparable ceramics and a three-level site hierarchy culminating in a site with at least 250 mounds (Joyce et al. 1989). Settlements in this area of Yoro, unlike those east along the coast or south on the Sulaco River, often include what appear to be Mesoamerican-style ballcourts. Unlike ballcourts farther west, which typically have a north-south orientation, most of these peripheral ballcourts are oriented east-west.

*Later Period V to Period VI: Terminal Classic
and Postclassic Periods*

The last two centuries of Period V, labeled Terminal Classic or Early Postclassic at different sites, were a time of transition throughout Honduras. Fundamental changes took place in the nature of settlements and material culture in Honduras. While many Period V sites were abandoned, others, including Cerro Palenque, continued in use with changes in material culture, especially ceramics. The occupation of these sites often extends across the arbitrary boundary between Periods V and VI.

One of the most striking developments in Period VI was a shift from the use of low platforms to support residential structures, back to on-ground construction. As a result, in most areas of Honduras, new Period VI sites are harder to detect. At the end of the period, written documentation from the Spanish Conquest is available to complement archaeological research, suggesting the existence of many more sites than have been confirmed archaeologically.

Among the sites which continued to be occupied into late Period V or early Period VI were Copan, Cerro Palenque in the Ulua Valley, Gualjoquito in Santa Barbara, Los Naranjos on Lake Yojoa, and Las Vegas, Comayagua (Webster and Freter 1990; Joyce 1985; 1986; Schortman et al. 1986; Sheptak 1985; Baudez and Becquelin 1973; Stone 1957; Baudez 1966). In Santa Barbara, on Lake Yojoa, and in Comayagua the use of Period V polychromes ceased, but new white-slipped polychromes and imported Plumbate ceramics were used. Polychrome ceramics were also abandoned at Cerro Palenque, replaced by a unique local tradition of fine-paste, unslipped, plastic-decorated ceramics.

In the contemporary Naco Valley (Urban 1986a; 1986b), a Late Classic phase lasting from AD 775 to 950 saw only minor change in ceramics, including the addition of a new fine-line local polychrome. The major center, La Sierra, continued to be occupied, and changes in settlement were minor. The Early Postclassic phase which followed, dated AD 950–1100, witnessed a coarsening of local ceramics and a gradual transition toward Late Postclassic types, while settlement essentially continued uninterrupted the patterns of the Terminal Classic.

Copan, long believed to have been abandoned around AD 800, also seems to have witnessed continued occupation in the Terminal Classic Period. Scattered finds of ceramic vessels of Terminal Classic type around the Acropolis, including early Plumbate, Salvadoran Delirio Red-on-white, and spiked censers indicate that use of the area by an elite with long-distance contacts continued during this period (Joyce 1986). A possible residential midden near Structure 22 and a tomb constructed in the east court, reusing very late sculpture, suggest these ceramics were not the result of activities of casual pilgrims, but of residents.

Results of excavation in the newly discovered second ballcourt of

Copan (Fash and Lane 1983) may also support the definition of a late continuation of use of Copan by an elite with radically transformed material culture. This ballcourt yielded sherds of Terminal Classic ceramics, both fine paste and Plumbate, as well as abundant examples of small obsidian points-on-blades of Terminal Classic form. Similar points were found at contemporary sites near Lake Yojoa and at Cerro Palenque. Many of the lithics from the new ballcourt were made of green obsidian which circulated from Central Mexico at this time. Green obsidian also formed part of the assemblage at contemporary Gualjoquito. The final construction phase fill of this ballcourt included Terminal Classic ceramics, although these were interpreted by the excavators as accidentally incorporated after abandonment.

Outside the main architectural group, evidence for continued occupation of the Copan Valley is gradually accumulating. In the surrounding elite residential zones, at least two burials incorporated Pabellon Modeled-carved vessels (Ashmore 1988:15, Plate II; Whittington 1989). Obsidian hydration dating applied to excavated samples from the surrounding valley suggests an even longer period of continuation of occupation than seems indicated by this evidence (Webster and Freter 1990). These rural settlements may have continued to be occupied by people making and using versions of the indigenous ceramics until well after AD 1000.

East of the Ulua-Yojoa-Comayagua corridor, the Sulaco Valley was apparently abandoned in early Period VI (Hirth 1982:63–65; Hasemann, Dixon and Yonk 1982:35; Benyo 1986:600–612; Lara Pinto and Sheptak 1985; Robinson, O'Mack, and Loker 1985). On the northeast coast, a sharp shift in all domains of culture marks the change from Period V Selin to Period VI Cocal culture which continued until the Spanish Conquest (Healy 1978a; 1978b; Epstein 1957).

Elsewhere, the surviving sites of early Period VI were soon abandoned. The late Period VI culture of the Naco Valley, which extended east into the western edge of the Ulua Valley, was a resurgence from a low point (Urban 1986a; 1986b). New painted ceramic traditions emphasizing new forms, motifs, and surface treatment suggest ties both to the contemporary Highlands of Guatemala and to Nicaragua (Wonderley 1981; 1984b; 1984c; 1985; 1986a; 1986b; 1987; 1988). Few other late Period VI sites are known. Research in Santa Barbara specifically designed to locate contact-period sites (Weeks, Black, and Speaker 1987) has identified a number of places mentioned in Spanish documents, and survey in the Ulua Valley has located late sites with ties to the Naco Valley (Wonderley 1984c; 1985).

Summary

Ongoing research in Honduras will undoubtedly modify much of this overview. Nonetheless, certain regularities seem likely to hold. The earliest settled occupation in Honduras dates to the Middle Formative, when widespread contacts with northern Mesoamerica are suggested by ceramic decoration and greenstone artifacts. Nevertheless, within Honduras this period was one of regional diversity. Although houses appear to have been built directly on ground level, the Middle Formative witnessed the construction of several large structures of presumed nonresidential use. No more than two kinds of sites, perhaps forming a simple two-level hierarchy, are known in any region.

During the Late Formative Period, a series of closely related decorated ceramics developed across Honduras and El Salvador, reducing the impression of regional diversity. While more sites with large-scale construction date to this period, there is still no evidence to suggest that residential structures were commonly constructed on low platforms. This innovation marks the beginning of the Early Classic, although most Early Classic sites are obscured by later construction. At the same time, the Late Formative structures in several areas were abandoned and left virtually intact, often within later sites. Unfortunately, the dividing line between Periods IV and V does not align with this major settlement shift, but rather marks a later set of ceramic changes.

Period V, the Polychrome or Late Classic Period, is the peak of apparent population development in Honduras. Nevertheless, it is clear that most Period V sites were established in late Period IV. Even the proposed marker for Period V, the development of local polychromes, actually began in late Period IV. However, Period V polychromes were strongly influenced by Lowland and Highland Maya polychrome styles. The settlement pattern of Period V is marked by the emergence of multilevel hierarchies, in most areas composed of three tiers, with the public architectural centers sometimes incorporating Mesoamerican-style ballcourts. Late Period V witnessed the transformation or collapse of these centers and their associated settlement systems.

Period VI encompassed both the dissolution of the Classic pattern and the development in the Late Postclassic of new centers. A return to the Formative Period norm of constructing houses on ground level rather than on low platforms is notable, and may have led to the underrepresentation of sites of this period in surveys. That such underrepresentation has occurred is clear from the contrast between early Spanish descriptions of Honduras and archaeological data.

Cerro Palenque occupies a place at the strategic transition from Late Classic Period V to Postclassic Period VI. Recent archaeological research at this site, and in the Ulua Valley in general, further clarifies its position.

The Prehistory of the Ulua Valley

Ulua Valley prehistory has been illuminated by research beginning in the 1890s (Gordon 1898b; Popenoe 1934; Strong, Kidder, and Paul 1938; Stone 1941), but the current understanding of this region owes most to the Proyecto Arqueológico Sula (PAS) of the Instituto Hondureño de Antropología e Historia (IHAH). IHAH encouraged a series of projects starting with the excavations of Nedenia Kennedy (1978; 1980; 1981; 1982b) at Playa de los Muertos and James Sheehy at Travesía (Sheehy 1978; 1982; Sheehy and Veliz 1977) and Choloma (Sheehy 1976; 1979). A program of survey and excavation at the site of Curruste (Hasemann, Van Gerpen, and Veliz 1977) was organized by IHAH personnel. Explorations in 1978 in the cane fields being developed around the site of Travesía (Robinson, Hasemann, and Veliz 1979; Lincoln 1979) identified the need for immediate survey and salvage, an impetus which became the basis of the formation of the Proyecto Arqueológico Sula in 1979.

The Proyecto Arqueológico Sula (PAS) to date has conducted a full survey of the valley using 1 : 20,000 scale air photos (Sheptak 1982), on-ground survey of over 15 percent (Pope 1985 : 110) of the 2,500-square-kilometer valley area, and excavations in both deeply stratified sites and complex architectural centers (Henderson 1984; Joyce 1983; 1985; Joyce and Sheptak 1988; Maschner 1982; Pope 1985; Robinson 1982; Wonderley 1984b; 1984c; Wonderley and Caputi 1983). The preliminary results of this project have been embodied in three dissertations and a preliminary report (Joyce 1985; Pope 1985; Robinson 1989; Henderson 1984), as well as unpublished project reports. PAS research has particularly illuminated three aspects of the precolumbian occupation of the Ulua Valley: the chronological framework, settlement patterns, and ancient environment and its impact on land-use.

Ulua Valley Chronology

The chronological framework is based on relative seriation of ceramic complexes, and external cross ties, reinforced by a few radiocarbon dates. Middle Formative Playa de los Muertos ceramic complexes (Kennedy 1978; 1980; 1981; 1982b), beginning ca. 600 BC, end at 200 BC with the transition to local Usulutan complexes of the Late Formative (Wonderley and Caputi 1983; Wonderley 1988; Robinson 1987; 1988). Late Formative ceramics have been described from the central floodplain and the eastern and western valley terraces (Robinson 1987; 1988; Joyce 1985; Wonderley and Caputi 1983; Sheehy 1976; 1979). Radiocarbon dates from Río Pelo (Wonderley 1988; Wonderley and Caputi 1983) place the Late Formative occupation of this site between ca. 100 BC and AD 100.

A very late Formative, or "Protoclassic," ceramic complex has been defined on the Chamelecon River (Joyce and Sheptak 1988). It contains Usulutan-decorated ceramics, Lowland Maya Ixcanrio Orange Polychrome, and ceramics similar to types from Early Classic Copan (Viel 1983), and should date to approximately AD 200.

An Early Classic ceramic complex identified underlying Late Classic components in the central valley and east valley edge (Joyce 1985; Beaudry, Joyce, and Robinson n.d.; Robinson 1987; 1988) includes Chasnigua Bichrome, a red-painted-and-Usulutan-resist-on-orange-slip ceramic group. Dos Arroyos basal flange polychromes like those published by Jeremiah Epstein (1959) remain rare, suggesting that these are trade items.

A minimum of three Late Classic Ulua Polychrome complexes have been defined (Joyce 1985; 1987a; n.d.; cf. Beaudry, Joyce, and Robinson n.d.; Robinson 1987; 1988). The earliest features fine-line, complex "Mayoid" Ulua Polychromes. The intermediate Late Classic complexes have Ulua Polychromes with simple bowl forms with geometric or animal representations, especially of monkeys. The latest Ulua Polychromes are again "Mayoid," with black backgrounds and human processional scenes. Comparisons of the Late Classic sequence with ceramic sequences from Belize, especially the sites of Altun Ha and the Belize River Valley (Sheptak 1987a; Joyce 1986; 1987a; 1988b; n.d.), suggest dates of AD 700–800 for the latest Ulua Polychromes and AD 550–650 for the middle Ulua Polychromes.

Throughout the central valley, these polychrome complexes are succeeded by a non-polychrome ceramic complex which is best known from the site of Cerro Palenque, and which defines the Terminal Classic through initial Early Postclassic occupation (Glass 1966; Sheehy 1982; Joyce 1985; 1987c; 1988c). These temperless, unslipped light yellow to orange paste ceramics (Tehuma Fine Buff group) replace the Ulua Polychromes, while local coarse paste jars continue with slight changes of form and decoration (Joyce 1985; 1987c; 1988c).

At Las Minas on the eastern valley edge (Robinson 1987:187–188) and at CR-331 on the Baracoa channel of the Ulua River in the northern valley (Pope 1985:44–51, 135; Joyce 1985:502–504), sites with ceramics affiliated to Early Postclassic Los Naranjos have been identified. Kevin D. Pope (1985:48) reports a single radiocarbon date (WSU 2899) from CR-331 of AD 1090±70.

The Late Postclassic Period is represented by a few sites, all riverine, on the western Ulua and Chamelecon, with ceramics related to the Late Postclassic of the neighboring Naco Valley (Wonderley 1984c; 1985). Anthony Wonderley describes the painted ceramics from these sites as locally made versions of the type Nolasco Bichrome, a red-on-white ceramic common at Naco. He notes that other ceramics appear to be distinct from those at Naco, and details of artifact inventories in the Ulua Valley (especially lower frequencies of painted pottery and of obsidian) are much different.

One of these Late Postclassic sites, Despoloncal, may be identified with a place named in the sixteenth century *repartimiento* of Pedro de Alvarado. A site (CR-337) near a second locality named in this document, Ticamaya, produced a single Nolasco Bichrome censer on survey, although limited excavations at the site recovered only Colonial Period remains (Pope 1985:70–73; Wonderley 1984b).

Ulua Valley Settlement Patterns and Land Use

PAS has also produced the first systematic data relating to settlement patterns in the Ulua Valley, which has been discussed in a number of preliminary reports (Joyce 1987b; Joyce and Sheptak 1983; Pope 1985; 1987; Robinson 1982; 1986). Settlement has been found to vary with geomorphological features, with the main river levees a focus of settlement throughout the valley's history. The valley edge terraces may have seen their initial occupation during the transition to the Late Formative (Robinson 1983; 1987; Pope 1987:103–112; 1985:177–182), or at the very least witnessed an intensification of occupation resulting in a greater visibility of sites for this period. The Late Formative is the first period during which mound-supported architecture was constructed, at sites such as Río Pelo (Wonderley and Caputi 1983) and La Guacamaya (Robinson 1982).

The Early Classic Period is difficult to identify in settlement data, in part perhaps because many of the sites occupied in this period continued to be used during later periods and are therefore categorized during survey as Late Classic. The ability to identify some Late Formative sites stems from their disuse and consequent preservation, in at least one case (at La Guacamaya) in association with a

Late Classic center. In contrast, no identifiable Early Classic sites are known which did not continue to be occupied during the Late Classic. Some kind of change in settlement organization between the Late Formative and the Early Classic may be indicated by this pattern (Joyce 1987b).

The Late Classic is the period best recognized in settlement data. Sites with Late Classic polychromes (although they may not be precisely contemporaneous, and may have been established in the Early Classic or Late Formative) are found in all geomorphological zones, including the previously unoccupied hills in the western backswamps. Late Classic sites use stone-faced platforms to support not only public, civic-ceremonial architecture but also residential architecture. An unanswered question is the degree to which Classic Period residential settlements without these telltale mounds have not been detected in survey (see Pope 1985 : 115). Such uncounted sites would increase estimates of settlement density and total occupation for the valley (e.g., Pope 1985 : 162–165).

Late Classic settlement hierarchies have been evaluated both on the east terraces (Robinson 1986) and in the southwest hills and central alluvium (Joyce and Sheptak 1983). Although details of the number of types of settlements vary between these analyses, both support the definition of at least two levels of sites with monumental architecture (including ballcourts) and a group of sites with nonmonumental architecture which can be differentiated in various ways. The presence of at least a three-level site hierarchy is evidence for the development in the Late Classic of complex political systems. The most complex sites appear to be relatively evenly distributed throughout the valley and are strategically located to control major routes of access on both the east and west sides of the valley. Smaller sites with public architecture are often spaced evenly between the larger centers.

Settlement data support the inference of a cultural collapse following the Classic Period. The Terminal Classic center of Cerro Palenque, which is described in detail in the chapters which follow, is the culmination of the Late Classic settlement pattern. All other late sites now known are relatively inconspicuous, lacking any identifiable public architecture, with structures lacking the supporting platforms of the Classic Period. The fact that all known Late Postclassic settlements are located on the river levees is in keeping with the distribution of identifiable sites named in the sixteenth century *repartimiento* of Pedro de Alvarado (Sheptak 1983). This document lists a number of settlements in the Ulua Valley, all of which are described as being on the rivers. It identifies the seat of the local chief,

Cisumba, as located on the river as well. Other sources describe this site as palisaded (Chamberlain 1953:34, 57).

The developments suggested by settlement patterns have been interpreted in light of the geomorphology of the valley in a unique study (Pope 1985). The ancient pattern of land use in the Ulua Valley appears to have been an adaptation to river-levee life, including both agriculture and exploitation of wild game and plants. It has been suggested that the Late Formative Period witnessed an actual demographic expansion resulting in colonization of the previously little-used valley terraces (Pope 1985:174–182, 1987; cf. Robinson 1983). Demographic expansion is also inferred for the Late Classic, with occupation of previously unused areas (Pope 1985:182–183). Several major shifts in the course of the rivers have been documented and given relative dates spanning the Formative through Early Postclassic periods (Pope 1984; 1985:43–74).

While the final results of the PAS are still pending, at present it seems clear that, as it was elsewhere in Honduras, the Late Classic Period was a peak of occupation and development of political complexity. The Formative Period underpinnings of this pattern are clearly related to widespread southeastern Mesoamerican developments (see Andrews V 1976; Demarest 1986; Demarest and Sharer 1982; 1986; Sharer 1978). The Late Classic appears to have been a time of both regionalization and intense inter- and intra-regional interaction, with links extending from Costa Rica (Lange 1984: 177–178) to Central Mexico (Joyce 1988b:277, 290). Relationships with the Maya Lowlands of Belize, whose beginnings are seen in the Protoclassic presence of Ixcanrio Orange Polychrome, continue through the Terminal Classic (Joyce 1986; 1987c; 1988b; n.d.; Joyce and Sheptak 1988; Sheptak 1987a) and are undoubtedly of major significance in the Classic Period prehistory of the Ulua Valley. Ethnohistoric accounts suggest that similar connections to the east coast of Yucatan were important (Henderson 1979; Chamberlain 1953). The data from excavations at Cerro Palenque illuminate these relationships and provide the basis for their interpretation in the concluding chapters. The next chapter describes Cerro Palenque, and my work there, in more detail.

Chapter 3. Research at Cerro Palenque

THE SITE zone of Cerro Palenque covers some 362 hectares in an area measuring 2 by 1.5 kilometers in the southwest Ulua Valley (Figure 3). Mound groups cover 26 hectares within the site zone, distributed in four clusters identified by separate site numbers. A small cluster of structures (CR-44, 1.9 ha), some with well-executed cut stone construction, is located on a 232-meter-high limestone peak overlooking the confluence of the Ulua, Comayagua, and Blanco rivers. This peak, Cerro Palenque, is the southernmost of a group of low, open hills in the floodplain.

Other architectural remains are found densely clustered on ridgetops in the 2 kilometers of hills which stretch north of Cerro Palenque, at elevations ranging from 40 to 100 meters above sea level. The central cluster, CR-157, includes a nucleated zone (13.7 ha) and peripheral groups (4.91 ha) and extends from the north side of Cerro Palenque hill to a steep crevasse on the north. Two smaller clusters on the west (CR-171, 2.17 ha) and southeast (CR-170, 3.33 ha) complete the site zone.

The hilltop site, CR-44, had previously been reported as one of the settlement centers in the valley, although no map or other information was available. The chronology, function, and relationships of Cerro Palenque were some of the issues targeted for clarification when the PAS began in 1979.

Early Research and Interpretations

Cerro Palenque first entered the archaeological record in Doris Stone's (1940:391; 1941:57–58) brief commentaries, based in part on the unpublished work of Dorothy Popenoe. Popenoe referred to her work at Cerro Palenque in 1927 in her discussion of Playa de los Muertos (1934). Unpublished photographs by Popenoe in the Peabody Museum pinpoint the areas where she worked. A few artifacts

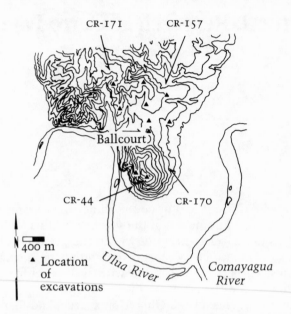

Figure 3. Cerro Palenque archaeological site zone.

in private collections in Honduras and at the Middle American Research Institute at Tulane University stem from this early research at Cerro Palenque.

Popenoe's photographs show massive cut stone balustrades, steps, and U-shaped drain stones, features still in place at the hilltop site today. The building associated with these features is part of a group which shows signs of major excavations, perhaps to be attributed to Popenoe. Excavation of a test pit in the plaza of this group was part of my work at Cerro Palenque in 1982.

Stone (1941 : 57–58), basing her discussion on Popenoe's work in this group, described the site as having crude masonry with thick stucco. She noted that it shared this feature with the site of Travesía, on the Ulua River farther north. Although Stone did not discuss the artifacts from Cerro Palenque in detail, among the collections of the Middle American Research Institute is a well-preserved Ulua Polychrome dish attributed to Cerro Palenque, donated by Stone. This dish is identifiable as belonging to the latest of the three subdivisions of the Late Classic Ulua Polychrome tradition. Two stone vessels approximately 1 meter tall, currently in a primary school in La Lima, Honduras, are also reported to come from Cerro Palenque.

These cisterns may be part of a drainage system which also included the carved stone drains encountered at the site. Finally, a carved stone slab from Cerro Palenque in a private collection in La Lima, Honduras, is clearly related to carvings from Travesía (Stone 1941: Figs. 49, 50), supporting Stone's (1940) argument for a special relationship between the two sites. A number of similar stone sculptures were recovered in my excavations at the site.

Stone (1941 : 58) stated that Popenoe considered the site a hilltop fortress, capitalized on for its strategic defensive location. This in turn supported an Early Postclassic date for the site, since increasing militarism was considered typical of this period. Cerro Palenque was consequently contemporary with Tenampua in the Comayagua Valley, also considered a "hilltop fortress" by Popenoe (1936). In fact, the two sites have some interesting parallels and significant differences (Dixon 1987; 1989 : 264–266).

While Stone's summary of the features of the hilltop site of Cerro Palenque and comparison of it with Travesía (1940; 1941) agree with my research results, her argument that Cerro Palenque was not a residential site is contradicted by my work. Stone based this argument on the lack of readily available sources of water for the hilltop site. In the parallel case of Tenampua, the large number of structures located (ca. 400 according to Boyd M. Dixon [1987 : 142; 1989 : 264]; cf. Stone 1957 : Fig. 3) clearly indicated that the site was residential, and possible reservoirs had been identified. While the total number of structures on the hilltop of Cerro Palenque itself is much lower, my research there has also produced evidence of a water storage facility.

Stone and Popenoe viewed Cerro Palenque as a fortress, primarily because of its location. Stone supported the special function identification with her argument against residential use of the site, based on lack of water sources. Unlike Tenampua (Dixon 1987 : 146–150), however, no clearly defensive features, such as walls, have been found at Cerro Palenque. While the steepness of the ascent to the site may in itself be a defense, the motivation for the identification as a fortress stemmed from the prevailing view of Maya prehistory. The Early Postclassic was viewed as a period marked by the warlike incursions of Mexicans (Stone 1969). In the Highlands of Guatemala, this model was supported by a settlement shift to hilltop locations (Shook and Proskouriakoff 1956), while in the northern Maya Lowlands, walled sites were built (Pollock et al. 1962; Lothrop 1924). More recent research in the Maya Lowlands has, of course, shown that warfare was a factor much earlier, and that defensive structures are not limited to a particular phase, but rather are found when and where the need arises, as for example in Early Classic Becan (cf. Webster 1977).

Cerro Palenque's hilltop location is in fact part of a widely distributed, though unusual, pattern in Honduras. In the Comayagua Valley the hilltop sites of Calamuya, Jamalteca, Maniani, Guasistagua, Chapuluca, Chapulistagua, and the better-known Tenampua (Squier 1870:76; Stone 1957:47–48, 50–53, 57–58; Lothrop 1927: Plate III; Popenoe 1936; Dixon 1987; 1989) are part of this pattern. In the Copan Valley, the hilltop site of Cerro de las Mesas was founded in the Middle Classic Acbi Phase (Fash 1986a:82). Along the valleys between Copan and Quirigua, the sites of Llano Grande, Agua Sucia, Los Achiotes, and Piedras Negras were described as located on hilltops, although these may be relatively low rises (Vlcek and Fash 1986). On the Caribbean coast, just west of the Ulua Valley, is the hilltop site of Tulian (Stone 1969:534). In the Ulua Valley, the site of El Zate (located by PAS) occupies an elevated pass in the next group of hills north of Cerro Palenque. Until these sites are investigated, we cannot assume they are contemporary with each other or of comparable function. Research at Tenampua and Cerro Palenque suggests occupation from the Late Classic to the Early Postclassic (Joyce 1985; Dixon 1987; 1989; Popenoe 1936). The hilltop center of Cerro Palenque lacks any signs of military function. Far from being solely a late site, the hilltop center was the original, earliest core of settlement in the Cerro Palenque site zone, which later spread to the lower, more open, less defensible hills north.

PAS Research at Cerro Palenque: 1979–1981

In 1979, Cerro Palenque was visited for the first time by PAS personnel, Project Director John S. Henderson and investigator Eugenia Robinson. Robinson's work in 1979 was a pilot transect survey from east to west across the southern valley (Robinson 1986). Cerro Palenque was included in one of her transects, and as it was a known site, a special effort was made to record it. However, the approach to the site from the town of Pimienta, to the northwest, proved to be long and arduous, and no mapping of the site was possible at that time.

My research at Cerro Palenque began in 1980 with a survey of the approximately 9 square kilometers of hilly terrain extending north from the peak. While another member of PAS, Dennis DeSart, carried out transit mapping of the known features of the hilltop site reported and discussed by Stone, survey teams under my direction scoured the ridge tops and valleys of the hill zone for what we expected would be small, scattered sites forming a peripheral settlement system around the known center.

To explain what we expected to find, we can consider the settlement pattern identified around the site of Curruste, located in a snug valley in the hills north of the Chamelecon River (Hasemann, Van Gerpen, and Veliz 1977). The central zone of Curruste has approximately 200 mounds, including large structures around a main plaza, probably public architecture, and groups of smaller mounds, presumably residential clusters. The survey carried out in the hills around Curruste center located a series of small, dispersed sites, some on ridges, one actually on a hilltop. These smaller sites, physically separated from the center and from one another, were living sites whose population would have supported the center, and looked to it for the special services typical of such villages in the Classic Period Ulua Valley.

Although we expected a comparable pattern around the hilltop site of Cerro Palenque, what we found instead was an almost empty zone except in the immediate vicinity of the peak of Cerro Palenque. There, each ridge top and all gentle slopes supported scores of low mounds. It was clear that we were dealing with a single, large, clustered site, which initial estimates placed in the same size range as Curruste.

We returned in spring 1981 to map this site with the greater precision of a transit. Expecting the 200 or so structures we had seen in the heavily overgrown fields in summer, we were astounded to find far more structures revealed by the dying back and clearing of vegetation at the beginning of the agricultural cycle. When we finally completed our mapping, we found that the site zone of Cerro Palenque, extending over a 1.15-by-2-kilometer area, included approximately 575 mounds (Joyce 1982). The large number of structures places it in a special class in the Ulua Valley.

The site of Cerro Palenque, as revealed by this mapping, consisted of four distinct clusters of structures (Figure 3). The original hilltop location, CR-44, was composed of three groups of structures on the highest ridge and two groups on outlying ridges (Figure 4). The main ridge runs southeast to northwest, with the central group at the highest elevation. There is reason to believe that a terrace on the southwest side of this ridge was artificially modified to form a link between the three main groups.

The southernmost group of structures at CR-44 is a single, rectangular plaza, as is the middle group, the location of Dorothy Popenoe's work. A test pit was excavated between these two groups as part of

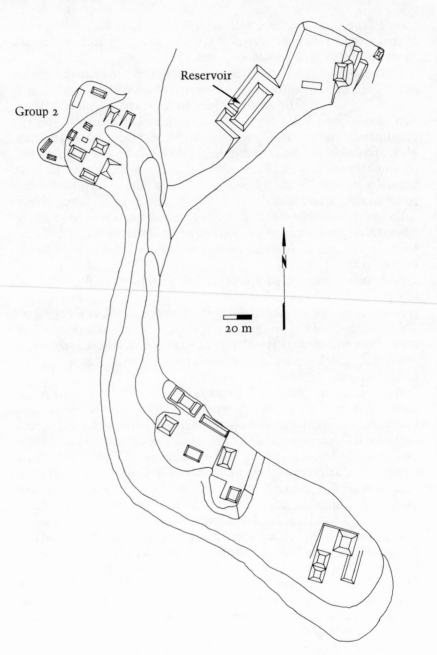

Figure 4. CR-44, Late Classic Cerro Palenque. Northwest ridge not shown.

my research. The northernmost group on the main ridge includes at least four small patio-centered mound groups, two tested in my excavations, on a series of terraces. From the north end of the main ridge two long, narrow spurs, perhaps artificially modified, run to the outlying groups of CR-44. Each of these is composed of a single rectilinear patio-centered mound group, but the northeastern spur also includes a very large depressed rectangular feature which is probably a built reservoir. Today, it has the appearance of a sunken courtyard, whose eastern edge is formed by the ridge joining this outlying group to the main ridge top. Two mounds built at right angles to this ridge, with top surfaces at the level of the ridge, define a 35-meter-long space. This sunken space is closed on the west by a long mound, with a slight step down on the southwest which appears to be a drain. From the western side of this feature, the hill falls steeply down ca. 200 meters to the Ulua River.

The hilltop site, CR-44, has abundant cut stone architecture, including massive block stairs, balustrades, and drains, including those photographed by Popenoe. Carved stone sculpture is also visible on the surface, and both the carved cisterns and carved stone slab now in La Lima came from this part of the site zone.

The bulk of the remains in the Cerro Palenque site zone, ca. 500 structures, comprise three clusters in the lower hills which extend north from Cerro Palenque peak. The largest and most prominent cluster, CR-157, crowns the highest ridge top, extending north from Cerro Palenque hill at an elevation of 100 meters (Figure 5). On the eastern slopes of the main ridge, small outlying mound groups which form part of CR-157 extend down to the 40-meter mark, close to what once was the bank of the Ulua River (cf. Pope 1985 : Fig. 2.7). Steeply falling slopes separate central CR-157 from a parallel ridge to the west, which is the site of a similar, although smaller, cluster, CR-171 (Figure 5). A final cluster located on the southeast flanks of Cerro Palenque hill, isolated from CR-157, is identified as CR-170 (Figure 6).

Each of these sites is composed of groups of relatively small, low, cobble mounds. These may be arranged in formal, rectilinear groups or less formal, looser groups around small open areas, or patios. Clusters of patio groups are also identifiable. In analyses of Maya Lowland settlement (Ashmore 1981; Tourtellot 1983a; 1983b, 1988) similar groups of small mounds arranged around patios have been identified as the residential units of sites, an interpretation adopted for Cerro Palenque.

Certain larger, taller mounds are located around open areas larger

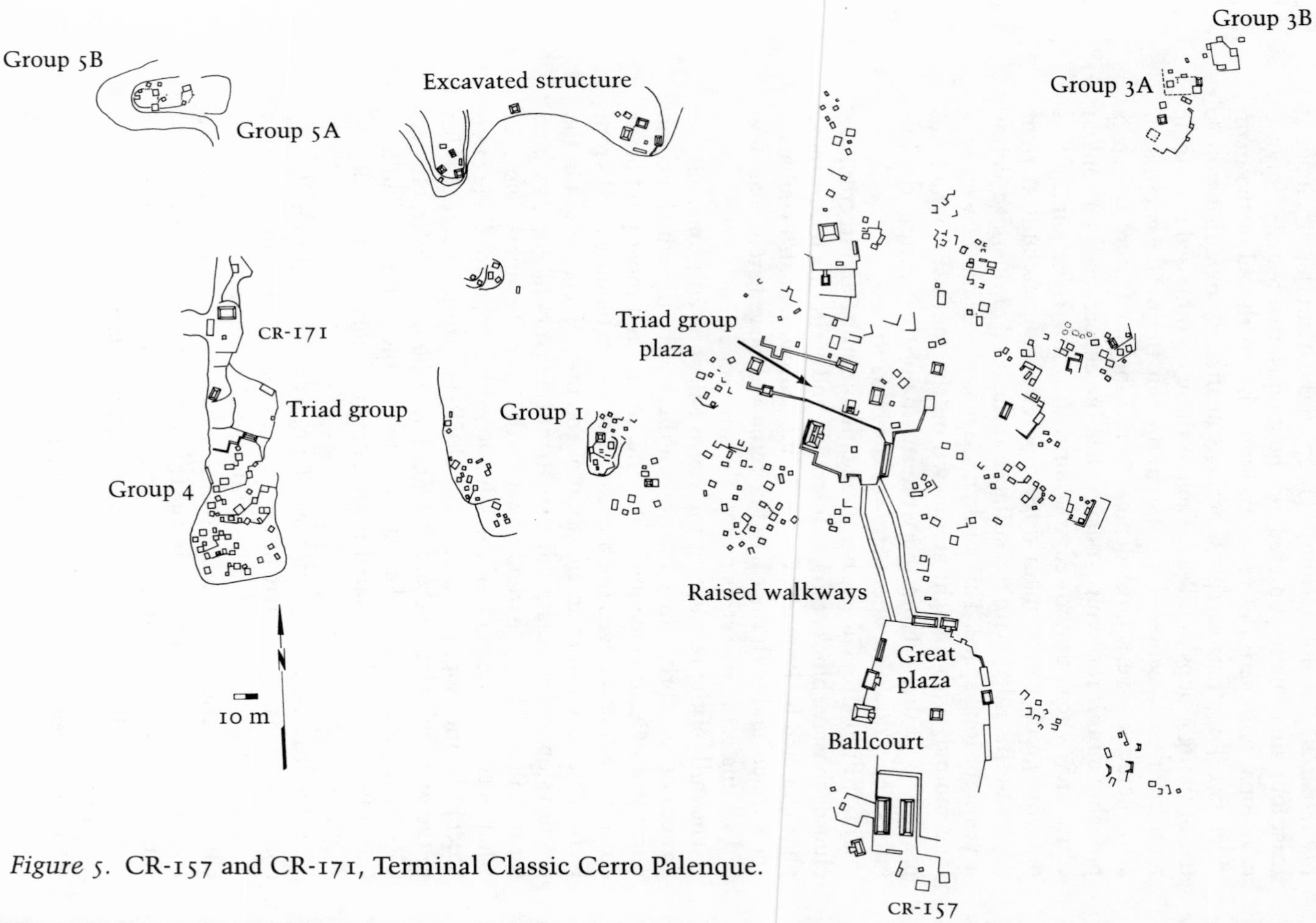

Figure 5. CR-157 and CR-171, Terminal Classic Cerro Palenque.

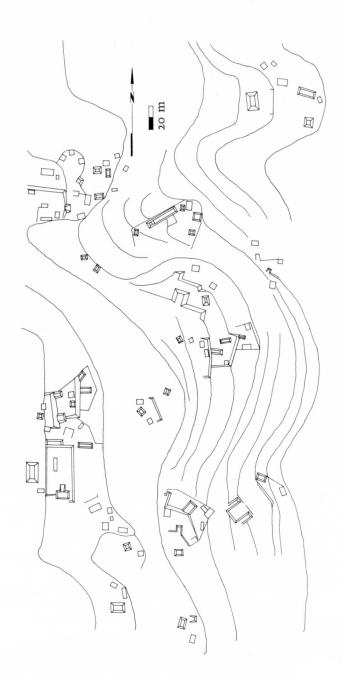

Figure 6. CR-170, Terminal Classic Cerro Palenque.

than the usual patios. Each of the four clusters in the Cerro Palenque site zone has at least one of these large plaza groups. The ridge-top spine of CR-157 is a series of plazas, with many unique architectural features including a ballcourt. The ballcourt formed the southwest corner of a plaza measuring 150 by 300 meters, from whose northwest corner extended two raised cobble walkways. These lead to a ramp on the south edge of a series of terraces, supporting plaza groups, rising to the northern edge of CR-157. CR-170 and CR-171 have a single, simple plaza group each. On the basis of excavation and comparison with other Mesoamerican sites, these plaza groups were identified as the public administrative, ceremonial, and possibly elite residential sectors of Cerro Palenque.

The results of survey and mapping indicated that Cerro Palenque was a unique site in the Ulua Valley. With almost 600 structures, it was much larger than any other site mapped by the PAS. Only the informal estimate of 1,000 structures for Travesía (Stone 1941) surpassed it, and PAS air-photo survey (Sheptak 1982) and later site survey (Joyce 1983) did not support this high estimate. The great plaza and ballcourt of CR-157 were the largest such features known in the valley. Excavations at Cerro Palenque provided the information necessary to understand these differences.

Excavation and Analysis: 1982–1983

How special a place Cerro Palenque occupied in the Ulua Valley was revealed when excavations began in 1982. My excavations were designed to test a model of multiethnic communities which might be expected to characterize a frontier region. Robert J. Sharer (1978) had described the development of Chalchuapa, El Salvador, as representative of such a multicultural settlement. Henderson et al. (1979) had predicted that the Ulua Valley would be found to be a multicultural zone, perhaps with ethnic enclaves sharing major settlements. The presence of these enclaves in a single "multicommunity" would have facilitated exchange between the ethnic groups which bordered the valley.

In an ethnic multicommunity, different neighborhoods would be occupied by people with varied cultural heritage. This should mean that the pattern and kind of archaeological remains recovered in different areas within the site would vary. Cerro Palenque, as the largest site known from the Ulua Valley, was a likely candidate for a multicommunity. Its location in the southwest Ulua Valley promised proximity to a range of ethnic or linguistic groups, possibly including Lenca (southwest on the Ulua and Blanco rivers), Paya or Jicaque (east along the Comayagua), and Maya, or Mayanized, groups (north and northwest). In developing my proposal for research, I had outlined ten specific differences I would evaluate, ranging from sizes and arrangements of structures to types of fancy pottery in use, to identify distinct ethnic groups within the site zone.

So I began my excavations in a residential group, one near the largest structures of CR-157, which presumably formed the civic and religious center of the site. I subsequently excavated in residential groups in the hilltop center, CR-44; in outlying groups of CR-157, northwest and southeast; and in two areas of the western ridge-top site, CR-171. Plans to excavate a group in the southeastern site, CR-170, were not carried out, due to my failure to persuade the landowner to allow excavation.

Over the first two weeks of excavation, we found that the kinds of structures we were encountering were precisely what research elsewhere in Classic Period Honduran sites had led us to expect. The mounds were platforms to support buildings raised on top, which included such features as built-in stone benches. A small central platform, barely 35 centimeters tall, proved to contain an unusual stone monument and carefully buried figurines. But at the same time, none of the ceramics looked at all familiar. None of the highly characteristic Ulua Polychromes, or the well painted and incised red-on-natural jars, which typified Classic Period sites in the valley, were found.

Since the ceramics which were excavated at first came only from beneath the remains of collapsed house walls, it was possible to believe they were simply very worn examples of the types we expected. By the end of the first two weeks, however, we had isolated and were excavating a large concentration of broken ceramics, stone tools, and other debris from the surface of one structure. This primary deposit resulted from discard of broken household implements. And in this garbage heap, finally, recognizable links to Classic Period ceramics could be seen. Comparatively crude red-painted jars were included, clearly related to the Classic Period incised and red-painted type. And, in place of the bowls, vases, and plates of Ulua Polychrome ceramics, a series of dishes and bowls of a unique Fine Buff ceramic were uncovered. With these ceramics were stone tools made primarily of local chert, rather than the obsidian typically used at Classic Period sites.

This pattern was repeated in all but one of the residential groups subsequently excavated at the site in 1982. In the hilltop site, CR-44, excavation from the very beginning uncovered Ulua Polychromes and Classic red painted and incised jars, and large amounts of obsidian were present. Most significant, a test pit excavated in a flat area away from the mounds at CR-44 produced a sequence of deposits which changed from Ulua Polychrome in the lower levels to a mixture of Ulua Polychrome and the Fine Buff ceramics in the upper levels. It seemed clear that the occupation of the major part of Cerro Palenque was later than that of the Classic Period Ulua Polychrome sites of the valley.

Further evidence of this sequence was provided in one excavation at CR-157. Excavations testing the core of structures at Cerro Palenque in general were unproductive, encountering a solid fill of cobbles. Only in two locations were any artifacts recovered from platform fill. In one case, a handful of ceramic sherds from a thin layer of clay under a solid cobble mound was recovered. In the second case, a large sample of cultural remains from a fill incorporated in the platform of a major structure was recovered. This sample corresponded precisely to the uppermost levels of the test pit at CR-44, including a few Ulua Polychromes and a great number of Fine Buff ceramics. In contrast, the ceramics from excavation of the structure which this platform supported, and all the other structures in the same group, produced only the Fine Buff ceramics.

At the end of the 1982 field season, it was clear that Cerro Palenque was a two-component site first occupied in the Late Classic Period. Analysis of excavated materials over the fall and winter of 1982 confirmed this picture and assigned the later occupation to the Terminal Classic Period.

The difference in chronology between what we expected and what we found had one important implication for the original rationale for excavation of the site. The most distinctive markers of different ethnic groups I had expected were the highly elaborated polychrome ceramics, absent and replaced by Fine Buff ceramics in the Terminal Classic. The analysis of these ceramics suggested strongly that variation in their nature within the site was quite minimal, and in fact as my analysis proceeded, it seemed clear that most variation between excavated locations could be explained in other ways.

The radical, unexpected difference in time period between Cerro Palenque and other similar sites in the valley, combined with its large size, posed a new problem for interpretation. This was the nature of the process, or processes, which led to the development of a much larger and more nucleated settlement at Cerro Palenque in the Terminal Classic Period. The newly recognized issue brought with it a complication which I addressed by excavation during a short field season in 1983. I had not undertaken excavation in the great plaza of CR-157 in 1982. This plaza was architecturally comparable to others in the valley, and I assumed that like those it had varied uses directed toward the community as a whole, and supported by it. These uses, including civic and ceremonial activities and possibly elite residence, were not germane to my investigation of variation between residential groups within the multicommunity. Once the question of the chronology of the site's occupation and development became an issue, excavations in this area to determine when it had been constructed and used, and when abandoned, became essential.

If the civic center had been built in the Late Classic, earlier than the majority of the site, then the multiple Terminal Classic residences might have been the result of slow growth around the center. If the center had been constructed in the Terminal Classic, then the entire development of the site, with the exception of the relatively small hilltop group, would have occurred in the Terminal Classic, a time when the majority of public centers in the valley were in decline.

Test excavations in the great plaza yielded a large sample of sherds and lithics dating to the Terminal Classic period. The final confirmation of this dating was provided by the excavation of the ballcourt. Architectural fill contained Fine Buff ceramics and other types of the Terminal Classic period. A few sherds of extremely late Ulua Polychrome ceramics of the Tenampua class (Glass 1966; Viel 1978), typical of very late sites in Comayagua and at Lake Yojoa, were included. This confirmed that the Terminal Classic occupation of Cerro Palenque was contemporary with the latest Classic Period occupations elsewhere in Honduras. The profile of the ballcourt was identical to Early Postclassic ballcourts from the site of Los Naranjos, on Lake Yojoa (Baudez and Becquelin 1973).

In the following chapters, I discuss the artifacts recovered, their distribution, use, and significance. Descriptions of excavated groups will clarify these later discussions.

Cerro Palenque Excavation Summaries

We carried out excavations in nine patio groups, part of six distinct clusters within the Cerro Palenque site zone. One patio group was in Late Classic CR-44, one was in CR-171, and the remainder were in CR-157. Three investigated clusters had three or more patio groups, two had two patio groups, and one is a single patio group in a dense cluster. Thirty-one mounds were excavated in these clusters, providing the information for group by group descriptions. Although a discussion of the distribution of artifacts is reserved for the following chapter, the general nature of artifact features is described in these summaries (see Joyce 1985 : 127–230 for details).

Group 1

Located on a small knoll near the center of CR-157, Group 1 was the largest patio group in a cluster of four (Figure 7). Four mounds define a regular, rectangular patio oriented north-south. The largest, on the north (1.75 m high, ca. 22 m² summit), proved to be the substructure for a rectangular room with preserved cobble wall bases. Most of the interior floor space was taken up by a rectangular bench on the north side (7.5 m²). Excavation of the bench uncovered a cached, unused mano in the northwest corner.

A short cross wall divided the summit room into east and west cubicles. An entry was defined on the east by a basalt cut stone block step. A wide terrace on the south summit and narrower terraces on the west completed the architectural features of this building. No clear access to the summit was defined on the south, suggesting entry via the west from the boulder-reinforced terrace connecting to the group's western mound. This mound was a small cobble platform (0.3 m high, ca. 9 m² summit) with no preserved summit architectural features.

The third mound in this patio group, on the east, was a broad platform (0.75 m high, ca. 38.5 m² summit). On the summit was a well-defined eastern terrace, probably behind a less well defined structure with wattle-and-daub walls on cobble foundations. Access to the patio was provided by a series of boulder steps on the west. A low cobble line, or wall base, extended from the southwest substructure corner towards the southern terrace, presumably blocking access to the group. On the summit terrace a large trash deposit was excavated, east of the low cobble wall base.

The final mound in the group was a central, low platform (0.2 m high, ca. 9 m² summit). This proved, on excavation, to be an enclosure defined by well-shaped cobbles, a single line on east, north, and west, and a double line on the south. Centered on the south was a 75-centimeter-long chlorite schist block, which may originally have been set upright as a stela. Buried east and west of this stone were ceramic artifacts, one of several caches in low central mounds at Cerro Palenque.

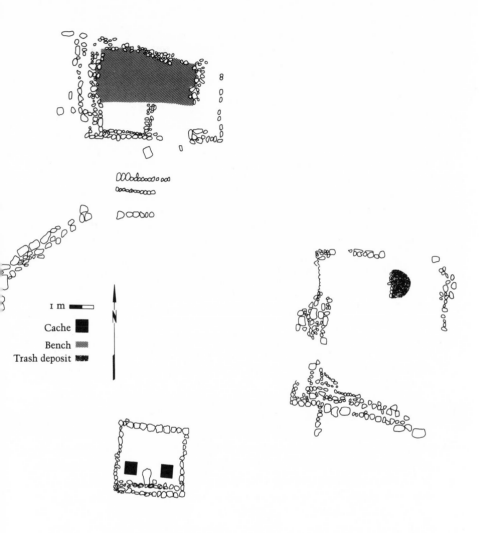

Figure 7. Group 1, CR-157.

Group 2

CR-44, located on the summit of Cerro Palenque hill, is made up of three ridgetops. The largest ridge supports two apparent plaza groups on the southeast, where a large stratigraphic test pit was placed. On the western side of the main ridge, at least four patio groups form a cluster. The most prominent of these was the second group we tested at Cerro Palenque (Figure 8).

The five structures investigated in this patio group differ in materials from those of Group 1, a point explained by the Late Classic date of this group. Nonetheless, certain architectural regularities are obvious, including the presence of one structure with a built-in bench, a central low platform with cached materials, and low terraces linking mounds in the group, closing off the patio.

The southwestern mound (1 m high, ca. 29 m² summit) has a cut stone substructure with plaster surface supporting a cut stone and cobble walled rectangular room with a large plaster surfaced bench (8.75 m²) on the southeast. The doorway and bench faced northwest across the steep natural slope, not northeast into the patio where access was provided by massive cut stone block steps. The remainder of the summit surface was a wide terrace, with a burned plaster zone on the northeast. Fragments of geometric and stylized anthropomorphic stone sculpture were found along the northeast substructure, and in the north interior corner of the room, apparently fallen in all cases from the upper façade of the building.

In the center of the patio, centered on the northeast-southwest axis of the southwestern structure, was a low platform (0.4 m high, ca. 9 m² summit) which on excavation proved to have two separate components. The earliest, oriented to the northeast-southwest axis, was a rectangular walled enclosure with a low plaster-surfaced platform built against the interior north side. The platform covered a pit, dug into bedrock and refilled. This feature was later buried under a cobble pavement, and a new southeast-northwest axis was defined by a series of cut stone blocks on the western exterior. Cached materials, discussed in the next chapter, were associated with both phases of this low platform.

Centered on the southeast-northwest axis of the patio was the southeastern structure, of a type without analogue in Group 1. A very tall substructure (2.15 m) supported two large rooms (18 m² each) joined by a single central doorway. The superstructure walls and floor were entirely coated by a thick stucco. The northwestern edge of the superstructure had been destroyed by looting, but the means of access was almost certainly a stairway constructed of massive cut

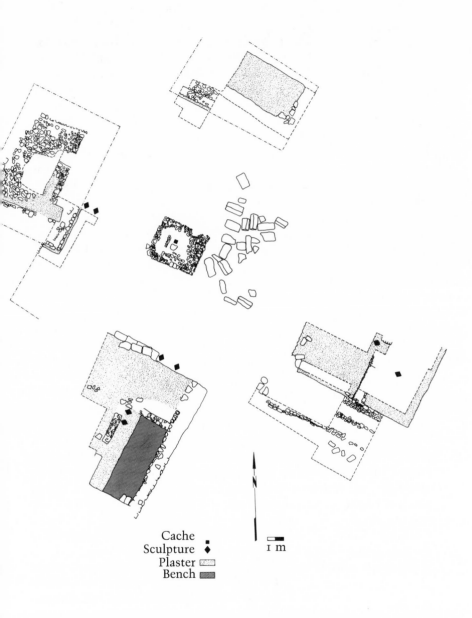

Cache ■
Sculpture ◆
Plaster ▨
Bench ▨

1 m

Figure 8. Group 2, CR-44.

stone blocks (found scattered in the patio) identical to those used in the southwestern structure. Sculpture fragments were found inside the summit rooms, in all cases above structural debris. Most were geometric, but one tenoned serpent head was also found. Like the fragments associated with the southwestern mound, these appear to derive from the upper façade of the superstructure.

The northwestern and northeastern structures shared a substructure façade with a sloping lower element (talud) and rectangular upper panel (tablero), an architectural feature common in Mexican archaeological sites. The northwestern platform (1.15 m high, ca. 6.4 m² summit) was constructed of plastered cut stone. The talud-tablero façade of the southeast side was continued partway on the southwest side to a short wall joining the northwestern and southwestern structures. Centered on the southeast side of this platform was a small cut stone block stair, leading to the well-constructed superstructure. This was a rectangular building with two rooms opening east. Both rooms have a flat stone paving covered by thick stucco. Two geometric sculpture fragments were found near the southeastern stairs.

The northeastern mound (1 m high, ca. 15 m² summit) had the least evidence of permanent architecture in this group. The talud-tablero façade of the southwestern substructure was of plastered cobble construction. The summit of this platform was covered in thick plaster, but no cut stone wall bases were identified. Fragments of wattle and daub and a short line of cobbles on the extreme east suggest a perishable superstructure.

Groups 3A and 3B

While Group 1 was located in the central zone of CR-157, Groups 3A and 3B were part of an outlying cluster on the northeastern edge of the site. We identified three patio groups in the cluster and tested two (the central, or Group 3A, and the northeast, or Group 3B; see Figures 9 and 10).

Group 3A is open on the south. West and north low platforms are built into the natural terrace. The largest, eastern, mound is composed of a low southern terrace and a high (1.2 m) northern platform (22.5 m² summit area). Excavation defined a rectangular cobble bench (9 m²) at the extreme north of this platform. Like the bench in Group 1, it incorporated a cache in the northwest corner: a stone ball and bar of unknown use. Well-preserved cross walls of wattle and daub on cobble foundations mark the east and west summit sides. On the packed earth floor south of the bench three small boul-

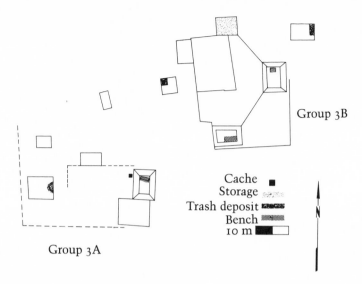

Figure 9. Groups 3A and 3B, CR-157: mapped structures prior to excavation.

ders cluster, perhaps the base for a perishable post. Access to this structure was apparently gained from the patio via the lower southern platform.

The western platform (1 m high, ca. 7 m² summit) supported a poorly preserved room with low cobble wall bases and a doorway on the east. A large trash concentration was found against the west side of the western wall bases. On the north the room was at ground level on the natural terrace linking the western and northern mounds of the patio group. The northern platform (0.75 m high, ca. 5.25 m² summit) also supported the cobble wall bases of a single small room with no evidence of access from the patio on the south.

Group 3B was northeast of Group 3A. A rectangular patio delimited on north, east, south, and west by mounds was further subdivided internally by well-preserved cobble and boulder terraces. The south and east mounds are joined by a diagonal terrace with a boulder ramp leading up to the northwest. Two cobble lines join at right angles to define the south and east sides of a smaller northwestern terrace, framed by the north and west mounds. A diagonal terrace joins the north and east mounds, forming a ramp down to the final, outlying, northeastern mound.

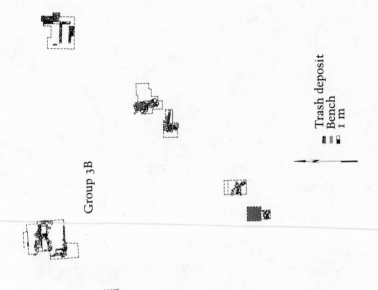

Group 3B

Group 3A

Trash deposit
Bench
1 m

Figure 10. Groups 3A and 3B: excavated structures following excavation.

Both the south (1 m high, 26.5 m² summit) and the east (1.3 m high, 29 m² summit) platforms support poorly preserved cobble superstructures. The south structure includes a cobble bench (6.25 m²) on the southwest and terraces on the north. The east structure has a smaller bench (3.9 m²) on the northwest and a cobble terrace on the south. Excavations into the core of the south mound recovered a handful of sherds in a clay fill at the original ground level.

The isolated northeast mound (0.75 m high, ca. 8.1 m² summit) was a platform supporting low cobble wall bases defining two parallel rectangular rooms opening west. A large trash concentration was excavated on the summit east of the eastern wall of these rooms. The north platform (0.5 m high, 19.6 m² summit) supported two small (ca. 1 m²) rooms with massive cobble walls. These rooms shared a common center wall and opened east and west. North of the rooms was a cobble terrace, where the in situ remains of very large jars were recovered.

The west platform (0.5 m high, ca. 11 m² summit) was formed by a series of terraces which ascended from east to west. On the extreme west summit edge was a single cobble wall base which extended the length of the summit.

While these were the only structures identified in this patio group, excavation of a low mound evident on the surface between Groups 3A and 3B delineated the corner of two wide, low cobble walls. One wall ran north-south, west of Group 3B; the other ran east-west, north of Group 3A. These walls may be boundaries of the cluster.

Group 4

CR-171, on the western ridge of the Cerro Palenque site zone, is a densely clustered series of patio groups south of a small plaza delimited on north, west, and south by monumental structures. The site was heavily overgrown, and the small structures excavated here were the worst preserved at Cerro Palenque.

On the western edge of the ridge, two mounds are located on the north and west sides of a patio defined by a cobble terrace east and south (Figure 11). Both mounds were eroding over the adjacent steep slope. The north mound (1 m high, ca. 20 m² summit) supported well-defined cobble wall bases forming the edges of a rectangular structure. A probable bench on the north side, disrupted by tree roots, incorporated small boulders and a cache of lithics and ceramic artifacts. Two ovoid ceramic effigies, one the head of a jaguar, the other a flying bird, and a needle-shaped object accompanied a chert

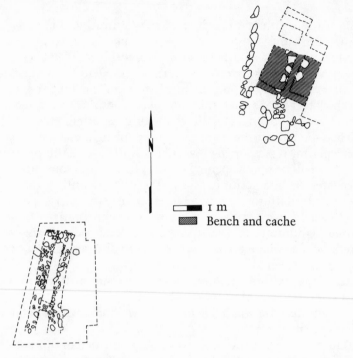

I m

▨ Bench and cache

Figure 11. Group 4, CR-171.

biface. The west platform (0.55 m high, 4.55 m² summit) was a cobble terrace, supporting a single long wall base on the extreme west. Mud plaster or daub was preserved on the wall base.

Groups 5A and 5B

An outlying cluster northwest of CR-157 composed of two patio groups on an elevated knoll was the site of our fifth group of excavations (Figure 12). Six mounds defining a small western patio (Group 5B) and a more complex eastern patio (Group 5A) were investigated. Boulder lines define two terraces on the east side of the eastern plaza. The lower terrace is delimited on north and south by small structures (*a* and *b* in Figure 12). The second terrace is marked by northwest and southwest structures (*d* and *e*) joined by a diagonal boulder terrace. The western patio extends from the southwest structure to a small western platform (not shown in Figure 12).

In the east terrace, the north platform (*a*; 0.85 m high, 9.6 m² summit) supported a single cobble wall base on the north. A large trash

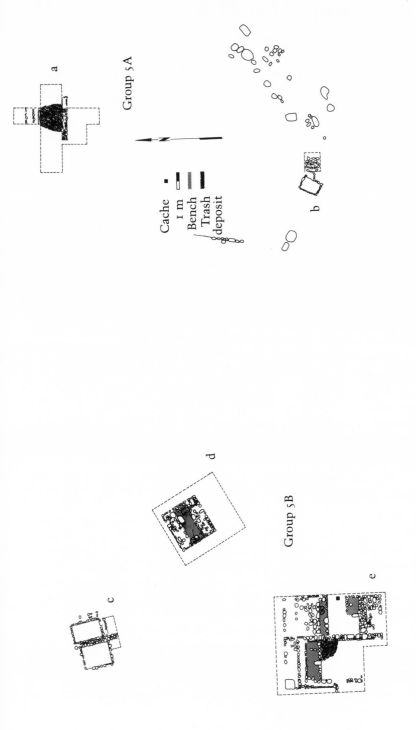

Figure 12. Groups 5A and 5B, CR-157.

concentration was located on the summit north of this low wall. On the south was a well-defined pit or room (*b*) only 0.5 m^2.

On the second terrace of the east patio, the northwest platform (*d*; 0.7 m high, 6.25 m^2 summit) supported a faced bench or wall on the north. Details on this structure, including the possible means of access, are scanty, since looters disturbed it while it was under excavation.

The southwest structure (*e*) was the most complex in this cluster, and included rooms oriented toward both patios. The eastern room (1.0 m high, 28 m^2 summit) was rectangular, with a rectangular northern bench (5 m^2). A narrow southern terrace provided access to the northern mound. A cache of lithic artifacts was located in the entry to this room. South of this room was a low terrace or outdoor bench.

The western room (ground level, 34 m^2 summit) was rectangular, with a rectangular northern bench (2 m^2). The floor of this room and the bench surface were covered with broken ceramics, most of which appear to have been intact vessels crushed in situ when the cobble superstructure collapsed. A ring of burned earth marks the northeast corner of the room floor. The doorway of this room faced a poorly preserved ground-level structure (9.2 m^2) on the west side of the western patio.

A platform (*c*; 0.45 m high, 3.8 m^2 summit) north of the complex southwest mound supported two rectangular rooms with a common north-south central wall and entry east and west. These rooms, which appear to pertain to both the western and eastern patios, had interior floor space of less than 2 m^2 each.

Groups 6A and 6B

The final cluster investigated at Cerro Palenque was on the eastern flank of CR-157, just above the old course of the Ulua River (Figure 13). Two patios were identified. The northern patio (Group 6A) was defined by a large, northern mound (*a*), a low central platform (*b*), and a long eastern platform (*c*) on the edge of the natural slope. A wide terrace (*d*) divides this patio from the southern patio (Group 6B), with a central platform, and eastern (*e*) and southern mounds. Not all structures in this group could be excavated.

The northern mound was a platform (1 m high, ca. 18 m^2 summit) with a well-defined western terrace and bench (3 m^2). Due to the natural slope, this platform was at ground level on the north. Excavation in the core of the western terrace uncovered a construction

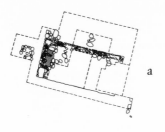

Group 6A

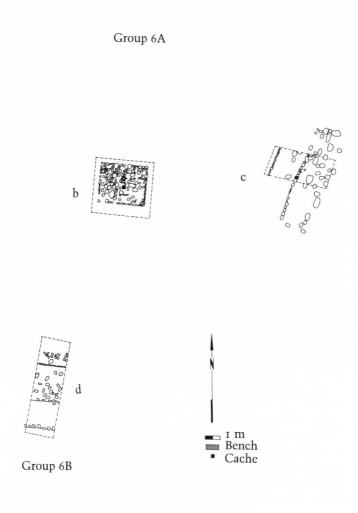

Group 6B

1 m
Bench
Cache

Figure 13. Groups 6A and 6B, CR-157.

fill incorporating abundant ceramics, lithics, and faunal material, unique at Cerro Palenque.

The eastern platform of the north patio (c; 0.35 m high, ca. 16 m² summit) was composed of a series of terraces rising from the west. No summit architectural features were preserved. The central mound (b; 0.3 m high, 8.6 m²) was a two-step terraced platform. Incorporated in the upper terrace was a cached biface.

A series of artificially modified terraces (d; 0.2 m high, ca. 8 m² excavated area) led down from the northern to the southern patio. The eastern platform of the southern patio (e; 0.85 m high, over 7.5 m² summit) was composed of a series of terraces rising from the west, with a rectangular room on the east summit. The central and southern mounds on this patio were not excavated.

Other Excavations. Our other excavations at Cerro Palenque in 1982 and 1983 included a stratigraphic test pit in CR-44, investigation of a tall isolated structure in CR-157 associated with a sculpture, and the test-pitting of the great plaza and ballcourt of CR-157. As discussed in later sections, these excavations produced distinctive artifacts that suggest these locations were not comparable to the residential groups represented by the bulk of the excavations.

We placed a stratigraphic test pit between the two largest, southernmost mound groups of CR-44 in order to recover evidence of the chronological sequence of occupation. Excavated to bedrock, the original 2-meter-square unit encountered no architectural features. An analysis of the ceramics recovered suggested that more than one chronological component had been sampled. A 2-meter-square extension of the original test pit uncovered a series of low walled cubicles, retaining an artificial fill. Below the footings of these walls were other ceramic and lithic remains, while the most superficial levels appeared to be above the constructed terrace represented by the cubicles and their fill.

We undertook the excavation of an isolated structure on the extreme north edge of CR-157 following the discovery of a displaced sculpted basalt column north of this mound. Excavation included the clearing of the southern façade of the structure, clearing of the summit, and sifting through backdirt from a looter's pit. The original location of the sculpture could not be determined, but both the artifacts and the building materials of this structure suggested a unique place within the site zone.

In 1983, we carried out a program of shovel test pits around the perimeter of the monumental structures ringing the great plaza of

CR-157 to provide information on their date of construction. We excavated a 2-meter-square stratigraphic test pit at the only location which produced substantial amounts of cultural remains. A uniform fill deposit was found.

At the same time, we laid out a 2-meter-wide trench on the center line across the interior alley of the suspected ballcourt on the southwest edge of the plaza. Sections of this trench which intersected the two flanking mounds were excavated, and the profile of the ballcourt was outlined. Built on a bedrock ridge, the ballcourt alley was flattened, natural rock. The alley was oriented north-south, and measured ca. 11 meters between the flanking mounds. These were approximately 35 meters long, and showed the mirror-image profiles diagnostic of Mesoamerican ballcourts. The eastern mound was located on the slope of the natural ridge, and an artificial fill had been incorporated to bring the surface up to level.

Preliminary Results

The first step of interpretation of the data recovered in research at Cerro Palenque was to establish the chronology of the site. Second, functional variation of different areas excavated was suggested by variation in distribution of artifacts and features. Together, these results paved the way for the next stage in interpreting the archaeological data. They made clear that although Cerro Palenque was composed of units identical in kind to those of Late Classic sites, the number of units and their scale were distinct from those of other valley sites.

Chronology

A relative chronology of occupation of Cerro Palenque was provided by the results from stratigraphic excavation, compared both with the ceramic sequence for the valley as a whole and with the content of construction fills and single-episode trash deposits. The stratigraphic test at CR-44 uncovered three distinct layers of deposits, unfortunately all from construction fill.

The most deeply buried material is comparable to Early Classic remains elsewhere in the Ulua Valley and contains the earliest ceramic types known from the site zone. A few sherds of similar ceramics were recovered from general debris in the southern structure of the patio group investigated at CR-44. This unique finding probably indicates that the initial establishment of this group dates to the Early Classic as well. These rare sherds, although certainly re-deposited, were not likely to have been transported a great distance up the hill slope from a floodplain site.

The second layer of material in the stratigraphic test pit includes abundant Ulua Polychromes of the early and middle complexes of the Late Classic Period, along with other ceramics diagnostic of these periods (Figure 15). This fill was contained within retaining walls built to form an artificial terrace. The majority of the remains recovered from CR-44 correlate with this fill. Subdivision of this long period of occupation is suggested by the two phases of the low central platform in the patio group excavated at CR-44. Although no diagnostic ceramics were included in these deposits, the materials cached in these two stages indicate dates in the Late Classic Period. The earlier cache, oriented to the center line of the structure with bench, was a single black obsidian eared biface. The form is one found in the Maya area during the Middle Classic Period of contact with Mexican cultures (Moholy-Nagy 1976; Rovner 1975; 1976). The later cache, which coincided with the establishment of a new axis on the center line of the nondomestic eastern structure, was a *Spondylus* shell containing a jade bead. This type of cache became common at Copan in the Full Classic, or Coner Phase (Longyear 1952: 110; Viel 1983).

The final layer of deposits in the stratigraphic test pit was quite distinct. It contained the later Ulua Polychromes not present in the lower levels of the pit; but it also contained Fine Buff ceramics (Figure 21). Examples of this type had been excavated from the riverbank near Santana by George Byron Gordon (1898b: Plate VII; Peabody Museum collections), at Travesía by Doris Stone (1941: fig. 54), and at Santa Rita by William Duncan Strong, A. V. Kidder II, and A. J. Drexel Paul (1938: 45–62; Peabody Museum collections). Their significance was first realized by John B. Glass (1966) who compared them to the then-recently described Fine Orange ceramics of the Postclassic Maya Lowlands. The Maya Fine Orange tradition consists of a number of distinct named styles, and Glass felt that the Ulua Valley fine paste ceramics were most comparable to Silho Fine Orange. However, the absence of painted decoration and prevalence of incised decoration suggests a closer relationship with Altar Fine Orange, a point first noted by James Sheehy (1982) in his analysis of examples from Travesía. However close these Tehuma Group ceramics are to Lowland Maya examples, they are distinct and probably of local origin, lacking a detectable slip, limited in forms and decorative techniques, and including at least one form rare or absent in Maya Fine Orange groups (Joyce 1987c; 1988c). The many links of this ceramic group to the Lowland Maya Altar ceramic group suggest a chronological placement in the Terminal Classic, in keeping with their apparent associations in the Ulua Valley.

Tehuma Fine Buff ceramics, and other associated types, were not found in the patio group excavated at CR-44. However, in every other excavated context at Cerro Palenque these ceramics were found. Their presence in construction fills at CR-157 suggests that this site was established during the Terminal Classic Period. In these construction fills, they are accompanied by occasional Ulua Polychrome sherds and other ceramics like those in the uppermost level of the test pit at CR-44. The polychromes and other types with roots in the Late Classic ceramic complexes are absent from the trash deposits and general lots excavated in patio groups in CR-157 and CR-171. The period of use of these patio groups represented by this in situ trash seems to be slightly later than the initial Terminal Classic. The superposition of this pure Terminal Classic ceramic complex over a fill representing the initial Terminal Classic complex in the excavations described above for Groups 6A and 6B supports this interpretation.

The occupation of CR-44, the hilltop center, spanned the period from the Early Classic through the initial Terminal Classic. The same period of occupation is indicated for a number of sites along the central river valley, including the architecturally similar site of Travesía (Joyce 1983; Sheehy 1978; 1982). CR-157 and CR-171 are unique to date in having been founded during the initial Terminal Classic, and nowhere else in the valley has a continuous transition from the initial Terminal Classic to a later phase of occupation been recognized.

Functional Variation

Initially, the division between larger and smaller mounds was assumed to relate to different functions. Larger mounds were believed to be public civic and ceremonial buildings or the residences of an elite class, while smaller mounds were expected to be common residences. Excavations supported the identification of the smaller structures as residences. Specific features such as benches provided evidence of possible uses of individual structures. The features documented in excavation provide the data to define different classes of structures, and the artifacts recovered provide the information to evaluate the activities carried out in these classes of structures.

Excavation in the ballcourt of CR-157 confirmed its special purpose, offering support for the interpretation of the great plaza as a civic-ceremonial precinct. Excavations of other large-scale mounds, one included in Group 2 of CR-44 and one isolated on the northern edge of CR-157, produced distinctive architectural plans and materials, and artifacts suggestive of nondomestic use as well. The detailed discussion of these features and their interpretation is the topic of the next chapter.

The research summarized above provided the data to explore the major questions originally of interest, even as the research focus inevitably changed. What were the social and political institutions of Cerro Palenque, insofar as these could be understood from the material remains excavated? What were the changes between the Late Classic and the Terminal Classic which accompanied the growth and nucleation of the site and the change in ceramics (from Ulua Polychromes to Fine Buff) and in lithics (from predominance of imported obsidian to local chert)? What processes resulted in these changes? Finally, in order to understand these institutions and their changes, how was Cerro Palenque linked to other areas around it?

Chapter 4. Social and Political Structure

THE SOCIAL and political structure of the living community of Cerro Palenque are no longer open to direct observation. The only available clues to these aspects of life in the community are certain kinds of material remains, buildings and artifacts. The interpretation of social and political organization from these bits of evidence is based on their arrangement and distribution throughout the site.

Social Structure: The Site as a Community

The first step in this interpretation is to define the limits of the site as a community. This was partly accomplished during survey, when we determined that the remains of buildings extended only throughout the 1.5-by-2-kilometer area defined as the Cerro Palenque site zone. Another part of the definition of the community was accomplished when the chronological framework of the site was worked out. This indicated that during the Late Classic Period, the community was small, limited to the hilltop area. During the initial Terminal Classic, this area continued to be occupied, but the larger plaza and at least some of the associated residential groups of the Terminal Classic site zone were added. During the latter part of the Terminal Classic (a time period estimated to be roughly equivalent to the beginnings of the Lowland Maya Early Postclassic), all or most of the Terminal Classic site zone was occupied, including the plaza, but the hilltop area seems to have fallen into disuse.

Cerro Palenque, consequently, was occupied during two distinct time periods, during which the nature of the community varied radically. Although excavated contexts provided bases to subdivide the Terminal Classic occupation into an earlier and later facet, for the majority of the site no such subdivision is possible without further excavation. Nonetheless, even if we ignore this differentiation and treat the entire Terminal Classic Period as one of fairly short duration, the definition of the limits of the community is still a problem. The zone with archaeological features may be continuous, but it is marginally possible that the site could be the remains of more than one community in close proximity. The solution to this dilemma is to examine the nature of the different parts of the site: what features are present in each zone, and do these duplicate or complement one another? At Terminal Classic Cerro Palenque, complex internal organization with some duplication of features, and presumably functions, but also evidence for unique functions integrating three sites within one community was detected.

CR-157, CR-170, and CR-171 are each composed of a series of smaller groups of mounds and clusters of mounds. Most of these mound groups measure 35 to 40 meters on their longest axis and are centered by patios 12 to 15 meters on a side. The mounds around these small patios rarely attain heights of over 2 meters or lengths of greater than 10 meters. In each of these sites, however, there is at least one group with taller, longer mounds grouped around an open plaza 50 meters or more in length. The interpretation of differences in function of these two kinds of mound groups and the structures which compose them provide the basis for viewing these three sites as part of a single Terminal Classic community.

Buildings and Their Analogues

Cerro Palenque as an archaeological site is a collection of approximately 575 collapsed buildings. Of these, 60 belong to the hilltop center which was the original Classic Period nucleus of the site, while 515 comprise the Terminal Classic site zone. Two major classes of structures can be defined, based on size and arrangement in groups within the site.

Monumental Structures. The first class is composed of monumental structures. These are buildings which are, even in their collapsed form, over 2.5 meters tall, and measure from 10 to 30 meters on a side. They occur in groups around large, open plazas, spaces 50 meters or more on a side. More rarely, monumental structures can occur in a patio group primarily composed of smaller structures. A single case of an isolated monumental structure was noted at Cerro Palenque.

Excavation of monumental structures was not a major part of the program of research at Cerro Palenque. Only three structures in this class were tested. The first was a single structure included in a residential group investigated in the hilltop center, CR-44. Of Late Classic date, it proved to be a tall platform supporting a pair of unusually large rooms. These two rooms lacked any built-in features and were almost devoid of artifacts. A few polychrome sherds and a significant number of sherds from a specialized form of vessel labeled a censer were the only ceramics recovered. Sculptured stone fragments were much more common, although all of these were found out of place, and must have been part of the upper wall or roof. The rooms were oriented along an east-west axis, marked by the interior door between the rooms, the exterior door of the western room, and the heavily disturbed massive cut stone block stairs on the west. The size and orientation of this building, and the artifacts recovered, suggest its identification as a specialized "group temple." Group temples are a recurrent feature of residential groups in other sites in southeastern Mesoamerica, such as Copan (Leventhal 1983; Gerstle 1985 : 105 – 108). They often incorporate elaborate tombs, and are interpreted as shrines to the founder of the residential group, venerated as an ancestor.

The second monumental structure excavated at Cerro Palenque was an isolated mound at the extreme northern edge of Terminal Classic CR-157. This was the only obviously looted structure in the entire site. At the north side of the structure, a carved stone plinth was encountered, a unique occurrence in the otherwise sculpture-poor Terminal Classic site zone. Excavation of this structure, including sifting through the backdirt left by the looters, provided a unique picture. The structure faced south, down a steep slope, and had a series of terraces or steps on that side. Constructed of cobbles, these terraces were faced with flat sheets of micaceous schist. This grey-green, shiny stone was not available any nearer than the northwest edge of the valley. It was used in only one other location in the site, as the material for a stone slab or stela incorporated in the central platform in Group 1, which had other evidence of ritual use. The summit of the isolated monumental structure was very small, occupied almost entirely by a platform composed of very large boulders.

The only ceramics recovered at this location were all pieces from a single, large unslipped modeled human effigy vessel. Fragments recovered included well-modeled hands, feet in sandals, and face. The person was depicted dressed in a feathered costume. This vessel was unique at Cerro Palenque, and not even a single sherd elsewhere in the site seems to represent such an effigy.

The unique carved stone sculpture from this excavation is closely paralleled by examples from the Late to Terminal Classic Puuc zone (Pollock 1980: 583). Called altars in that area, they are found at over 30 sites, often set up on small masonry platforms in front of important buildings. While the majority are simple round columns, rectangular examples were recorded from sites in Campeche, on the west coast of Yucatan. Both round and rectangular column "altars" can carry sculpted or incised geometric decoration.

Examples of square columns supporting a sculptured three-part molding identical to the Cerro Palenque sculpture were noted in Campeche at Xcalumkin, Yakalmai, Xcocha, Kanki, Maioch, Acanmul, and perhaps Bakna, although this example is not illustrated (Pollock 1980: 456, 490, 515, 529, 532, 537, 538; Figs. 763a, 866b,c,d, 896d, 902). The Campeche sculptures have diverse treatment of the area above the molding.

The closest parallel to the Cerro Palenque example is a column altar with an identical molding and rounded upper surface, found near the base of the main pyramid at the site of Mayapan (Shook 1954: Fig. 5b). Mayapan also provides the only parallel for the human effigy vessel found at Cerro Palenque, similar effigies in Mayapan Unslipped Ware of the type Hoal Modeled which were used in ritual (R. E. Smith 1971: 104–105, 196). Although the traditionally accepted dating of Mayapan places this type considerably later than the Terminal Classic (after AD 1200), Mayapan-style ceramics are present at Lamanai, Belize, before AD 1140 (Pendergast 1986: 240). The beginning of the Terminal Classic occupation at Lamanai (AD 900–950) is marked by construction of a ballcourt, incorporating a cache of liquid mercury attributed to Honduran sources (Pendergast 1986: 229), perhaps related to contemporary developments at Cerro Palenque. Charles Lincoln (1986: 189–190) has argued for an earlier placement of Mayapan, overlapping with Chichen Itza, consistent with the relations to Lamanai and the latest Cerro Palenque occupation. Certainly, the presence at Cerro Palenque of both an unusual stone sculpture and a modeled effigy vessel most closely comparable to remains from Mayapan suggests some kind of relationship, however attenuated. As at Mayapan, and in the sites of the Campeche zone, the sculpture and effigy vessel indicate that this building was a location for a ritual.

The third monumental structure tested was the ballcourt at CR-157. Two test pits on the inner edges of the two parallel mounds established the presence of the symmetrical profiles diagnostic of ballcourts. A number of studies (A. L. Smith 1961; Borhegyi 1969; Quirarte 1977) have established that the dimensions and profile of ballcourts vary over time and space in Mesoamerica. Stephan F. de Borhegyi (1969), using the broadest number of traits, included the entire area of western Honduras in a single zone with the Maya Lowlands. In contrast, A. Ledyard Smith (1961) limited his survey to

132 ballcourts from the highlands of Guatemala and the Motagua Valley, and considered only the architectural features of the court itself. Two types, the "open end" and "open end A," have features like the Cerro Palenque ballcourt. These types suggest ties to the Guatemala Highlands, a point reinforced by the ampler data provided by Jacinto Quirarte (1977).

The Cerro Palenque ballcourt had a low, horizontal bench, a vertical wall, and a sloping upper surface, a profile comparable to the Early Postclassic Río Blanco Phase ballcourts of Los Naranjos on Lake Yojoa to the south (Baudez and Becquelin 1973). Like the latter, the ballcourt at Cerro Palenque had a single stone disk set in the eastern wall as an apparent center-line marker. Although the construction was primarily cobble, at least the lowest terrace on the west was faced with small cut-stone blocks of rhyolitic tuff.

The profile and general plan of the Cerro Palenque and Los Naranjos ballcourts are shared by the open-end types of Highland Guatemala (A. L. Smith 1961:108–110). Markers on the sloping sides are present in both types, with the occurrence of a single carved stone (on the west) noted for the Late Classic open-end type (ibid.:102–104). The Postclassic open-end-A type differs in the lack of plaster, the presence of tenoned markers, and the possible presence of superstructures on the ranges (ibid.:108–110). The most important difference, however, is that one end of open-end-A ballcourts leads into an adjoining plaza group with a central altar-platform (ibid.:104–106), identical to the plan of Cerro Palenque's Terminal Classic ballcourt. Both types were widely distributed, from Huehuetenango and Quiche through Alta Verapaz. All the Late Classic examples are valley bottom sites, while the Postclassic examples are located on valley bottoms, slopes, and two "defensible hilltops" (ibid.:104, 108).

In contrast, the typical ballcourt of the Motagua Valley and western Honduras is the enclosed-A type (A. L. Smith 1961:114–116). Although usually this type has enclosed end zones, at least eight ballcourts from the Motagua drainage have the same profile but one or two open ends (ibid.:117–119). The profile is most distinctive, with a vertical lower wall supporting a sloping upper surface, exemplified by the Classic Period ballcourt of Copan. All of the examples are Late Classic in date.

Quirarte (1977) illustrates and amplifies the same relationships. Again, ballcourts from Guatemalan Highland sites of the Late Classic through Early Postclassic, such as Huil, Tzicuay, and Chijolom, are closest in profile, dimensions, and proportions to that of Cerro Palenque. The Cerro Palenque ballcourt does differ in one regard: the angle of its sloping surface, at 28.8 degrees, is significantly lower.

It compares favorably to the type modeled on Copan (25–30 degrees), essentially Smith's (1961) enclosed-A and Motagua Valley variant types. Also comparable in this regard are the ballcourts of Coba and San José, Belize. Quirarte (1977) characterizes these as derived from the Copan model by the addition of low benches on the alley, an interpretation also possible for the Cerro Palenque ballcourt.

These three structures exemplify what is presumed to be true of all the monumental architecture at Cerro Palenque. They have little or no domestic debris, and were used either for unique purposes or in ceremonial activities. The materials used in their construction are the most elaborate known in each site. Unique ceramic vessels were found in each case, and sculpture was either most abundant in, or limited to, these structures.

The ballcourt is a specialized form, dictated by the requirements of the ballgame. The other two excavated monumental structures are part of a subclass characterized by almost square bases and very tall sides. These conical structures are the only type of monumental building which occurs outside plaza groups. The floor plan of the structure in Group 2, with an interior room and an antechamber, is identical to the common Mesoamerican temple plan represented in both Maya and Classic Oaxacan sites (J. Marcus 1978). Around plazas, conical monumental structures may be accompanied by long, lower rectangular platforms. In size, plan, materials, and associated artifacts, monumental structures contrast fundamentally with the vast majority of structures distributed around small patios at Cerro Palenque.

Nonmonumental Structures.   The majority of the mounds at Cerro Palenque are under 2.5 meters in height. These nonmonumental structures are also usually smaller in length and width than monumental structures. Because the sample of smaller mounds is larger than that of monumental structures, and because they are the basic component of patio groups, which were the focus of my investigations, a larger number of these nonmonumental structures were excavated. All of the excavated nonmonumental structures provided evidence of domestic use. Groups of nonmonumental structures around patios, like the 103 examples at Cerro Palenque, are universally regarded in eastern Mesoamerica as the archaeological remains of residential groups (Ashmore 1981; Willey 1981; Tourtellot 1983a; 1983b; 1988).

In my analysis of the nonmonumental structures of Cerro Palenque, I detected successive, nested levels of settlement features. Individual buildings, groups of buildings around a common patio, and clusters of patio groups were all features of the site. My approach to understanding the uses of these settlement features combined archaeological, ethnohistoric, and ethnographic analogies with formal analysis of mapped features, supplemented by the information provided by excavations in a number of small structures.

The three kinds of comparative cases offer different degrees of information. Archaeological settlement patterns can be compared in formal terms, based on the structure of the material remains, but not on the interpretations proposed for them. Investigations of the Sepulturas zone of Copan (Leventhal 1979, 1983; Fash 1983a; Hendon 1987) documented the presence of a series of nested settlement units, ranging from the individual structure to the patio group and cluster. Evidence for ritual was present at each level, ranging from distributions of specialized artifacts to the construction of specialized structures.

Comparison with the archaeological example most removed, spatially and culturally, from southeastern Mesoamerica demonstrates that these shared characteristics are not some kind of regional peculiarity. Discussions of settlement at Teotihuacan, Mexico (Millon 1974; 1981), a densely occupied city, identify similar nested levels of settlement, each with evidence of ritual.

The ethnohistoric case of the Aztec capital, Tenochtitlan, provides a further example of the presence of successive nested levels of settlement, each with specialized ritual (Calnek 1976). Here, where archaeological evidence is limited, sixteenth-century documents detail the nature of settlement organization and make clear the crucial role of common ritual at each level of the community.

Contemporary ethnographic accounts also document the same kinds of features. Ethnographies add richer details, but the degree of attention to settlement organization is quite variable in these sources. For example, George Foster (1967: 32–34, 48–51, 55–57) alludes to similar patterns in Tzintzuntzan, a Tarascan-speaking town in Michoacan, Mexico. The typical household is composed of several buildings around a private courtyard, with the kitchen housed in a separate building. Joint households, composed of more than one married couple, account for one-fifth of the population. Some of these joint households share cooking, others separately use the same kitchen, while a minority, with separate kitchens, are joint only because they share the house site. Because Foster's interests do not center on settlement pattern, his description is quite spare. In particular, he does not consider the role of ritual in the definition and maintenance of the household, a topic central to my interpretation of Cerro Palenque.

A study of the Chorti Maya of western Guatemala (Wisdom 1940) provides the necessary scale of analysis, although description of many topics of potential interest is limited. Both the necessary scale and detailed description are furnished for the Tzotzil Maya community of Zinacantan, Chiapas (Vogt 1969). These two ethnographic cases provide general guidance in interpreting the meaning of variation within the settlement of Cerro Palenque. The features common to these two cases, used as a basis for comparison with Cerro Palenque, clearly are applicable more generally within Mesoamerica, although much less well documented. Their presence in widely dispersed, unrelated societies documented through archaeology, ethnohistory, and ethnography suggests that these features are part of a pattern typical of Mesoamerica.

In the ethnographic examples, the largest structure in a household group is the main house, where people sleep and carry on most other activities (Wisdom 1940:119–138; Vogt 1969:71–91). Assuming that the same relationship of space utilization held true at Cerro Palenque, and that the largest building in a group was most likely to have been used as a general residence, I tabulated the basal dimensions (rounded to the nearest 2.5 m of length) of the largest nonmonumental structure on each patio. I separately tabulated the measurements of the second-largest and remaining smaller structures in each group (Table 1). Most groups had no more than three structures. In those with more structures, overlapping ranges were noted in the sizes of the smallest structures, and they have been grouped in the table.

Two peaks are evident in the size range of largest structure within each patio, one at approximately 49–50 square meters, one at approximately 100 square meters. The majority of largest structures have basal areas clustered around these peaks. Thirty-eight of the largest structures are approximately 7.5 by 7.5 meters or 5 by 10 meters, an approximate area of 49 to 50 square meters. Another 12 have a basal area of approximately 100 square meters. Eighty percent of the largest structures have basal dimensions over 45 square meters. Patios with very small structures are generally part of clusters which include at least one patio group with structures over 45 square meters in area.

Other regularities are presented by the distribution of areas of the second-largest structure in each group. In 46 patios, the basal area of

Table 1. *Structure size and relative position in patio group*

Basal Dimensions (square meters)	Largest Structure in Group	Second-Largest Structure in Group	Third- to Sixth-Largest Structure in Group	Totals
		Frequencies of:		
Over 100	7	1		8
100	12	7		19
90	1			1
84	4			4
80		1		1
75		1		1
72	1		1	2
70	6	3	1	10
64	6	2		8
63	1			1
60	3			3
50	22	12	5	39
49	16	19	9	44
45	2			2
42	3			3
40	1			1
36	2	13	20	35
35	4	6		10
32	2			2
30	4	3		7
28		2	2	4
27		1		1
25	2	23	66	91
24	3	1	2	6
21		2	6	8
20	1	6	5	12
18		2		2
16		3	2	5
15		1	11	12
12		1	3	4
8			1	1
6			1	1

Excluding structures over 2.5 m in height, terraces with a single defined dimension, ramps, and other features.

the second-largest structure is 49 square meters or more. In the majority of the patio groups, the second-largest structure had a smaller basal area, with peaks centered around 24–25 square meters (24 examples) and 35–36 square meters (19 examples).

The same peaks are evident in the remaining structures. Ten patio groups had additional structures with basal dimensions 49 square meters or more. The majority of smaller structures in patio groups fell into the smaller size range, with notable peaks at approximately 36 square meters (20 examples) and 24–25 square meters (68 examples).

A total of four classes of structures were identified by this combination of relative size within a patio group and absolute basal dimensions. Modal dimensions of 25, 35, 50, and 100 square meters defined these four classes. The largest and often the second-largest structures in each group fell into the top two dimension classes. At least one structure belonging to the smaller classes was typically part of each group.

Differences in use of the larger and smaller structures incorporated within single groups are suggested by both ethnographic analogy and archaeological data. The Chorti Maya house groups include two classes of buildings (Wisdom 1940: 123–125). Kitchens and dormitories typically measured 20 by 12 feet (approximately 23 sq m). Storage houses, sheds, and temporary structures typically measured only 10 by 8 feet (approximately 7.5 sq m). Although the precise dimensions and ratios are specific to this case, the division between larger and smaller structures with distinct uses seems consistent with evidence from excavated small structures at Cerro Palenque.

When the 32 structures from patio groups which had been excavated at Cerro Palenque were grouped according to the size classes defined, an interesting pattern emerged. The larger classes (50 and 100 sq m) included all excavated structures with built-in benches. The floor space inside these structures ranged from 17 to 34 sq m. Other structures in the 50-square-meter class lacking benches but with remains of low house walls and trash concentrations had interior floor areas ranging from 26 to 38 square meters. The overlapping interior floor space measurements confirm the inclusion of both kinds of structures in a single class based on dimensions. The major difference between these two kinds of structures is the presence of benches, which contrasts with the presence of trash concentrations. In the ethnographic examples, kitchen areas were sometimes separated from the main house, the residence of the lineage head. The complementary distribution of trash which stems from food preparation and benches suggests a similar relationship at Cerro Palenque.

Structures in the smaller size classes which were excavated had less interior space and many specialized features. Structures in the 35-square-meter basal dimension class were platforms supporting at most single wall bases and little debris. Their summit area ranges from ca. 4 to 20 square meters, although the majority (10 of 12) are between approximately 4 and 10 square meters. The smallest structures had specialized features such as very small rooms and remains of large storage jars, caches, or monuments. Five of the seven excavated structures in this class had outside dimensions of approximately 9 square meters. Distributions of artifacts discussed below suggest different and more specialized uses of these very small nonmonumental structures.

The differences between monumental structures serving specialized, nondomestic functions and small structures exhibiting evidence of a diversity of residential activities suggest that patio groups are homesteads and plazas are civic-ceremonial centers (probably incorporating residence of an elite). The argument for the integration in a single community of Terminal Classic CR-157, CR-170, and CR-171 rests on the presence in CR-157 of unique monumental architectural complexes which must have served the entire settlement.

One Community or Three?

Each of the three sites has a number of comparable patio-centered groups, the minimal residential units. Hence none of the sites was an exclusively special-function settlement. In addition, each of the sites has one or more monumental plazas with special-purpose, civic-ceremonial architecture. In these features, unlike the residential units, there are pronounced differences between the three sites.

CR-170 and CR-171 each have a single plaza, 50 meters on a side, delimited by conical mounds on the north, west, and south. This triadic structure is superficially similar to one that has been noted in sites in the central Maya Lowlands (Ashmore 1986; 1989), but as Kenneth Hirth (1988:323) notes, the directional orientation differs in Honduran examples, and consequently the cosmological significance of the pattern must have been reinterpreted. The open eastern side of the main plaza at CR-171 faces, and appears to be oriented toward, a prominent structure in the monumental architectural zone of CR-157. The open eastern side of CR-170's plaza faces the floodplain and course of the Ulua River.

While the plaza groups of CR-170 and CR-171 appear to duplicate

each other, they are distinct from CR-157. The monumental architectural zone of CR-157 is more complex. It includes four separate
components that extend along the highest ridgetop: the ballcourt
complex, on the southwest; the great plaza; the series of terraces
connected to the great plaza by walkways; and a unique isolated
conical structure on the extreme north. None of these features is
like the triadic groups of CR-170 and CR-171, and neither of these
sites has features of this kind.

The monumental architectural zone of CR-157 may be suspected
of having served different functions from the plazas of CR-170 and
CR-171. Indeed, the ballcourt served a known function: an arena for
the ritually significant ballgame, as well as a feature marking the
boundary between sacred and profane space in the site plan (Ashmore
1986; 1989; Gillespie 1985). The oversized patio-centered group on
the extreme southern edge of the ballcourt, the defining feature of
the "open-end-A" type of ballcourt (A. L. Smith 1961:102–110),
should have been an elite residential group, according to one model
(Ashmore 1986; 1989).

The great plaza differs not only in scale (150 by 300 m) but also in
composition from the plazas of CR-170 and CR-171. The plaza is
closed on west, north, and east by both conical structures and long
linear platforms. A conical structure is centered in the plaza. The
southern side of the plaza, with the exception of the ballcourt, is
open. The combination of structures suggests more complex and
varied uses than the small east-facing triadic plazas of CR-170 and
CR-171. While only three sides of the rectangular plaza are defined
by mounds at all three sites, the number and variety of structures is
higher for the great plaza of CR-157, and the open southern side is
transformed by the addition of the ballcourt. The great plaza more
strongly recalls the triadic pattern identified at Lowland Maya sites,
sharing the open southern exposure. The ascending terraces north
of the great plaza are also open on the south side.

The great plaza is joined on the north by parallel walkways to a
series of terraces which support monumental architecture. Triads of
structures on these terraces, conical mounds and long flanking platforms, define rectangular courts open on the south. The orientation
and combination of types of structures in these courts closely reflects the planning of the great plaza, and recalls in size and form
(although not in orientation) the triad groups at CR-170 and CR-171.

Finally, on the extreme north, a unique isolated conical structure
was located. As noted in the description of excavations at this looted
site, the structure consisted of a series of terraces or steps which

faced south, finished with flat sheets of micaceous schist. Placed on the edge of the steep ridge slope, this structure is oriented visually toward the peak of Cerro Palenque. The series of terraces which define its southern face lead down the slope. Its small summit platform lacked all signs of walls, and at some time the structure had featured a carved sculpture. All of these features confirm its distinction, but leave its precise use uncertain. Whatever function it had was unduplicated in either CR-170 or CR-171.

The unique forms, and presumably functions, of these features of CR-157 would only have been available to the population of CR-170 and CR-171 if they were part of a single community supporting this center. Another line of analysis supports this interpretation. In the southeast Ulua Valley, Robinson (1983) found a regular relationship between the number of small structures (and presumably the population) of a settlement area and the mass of the monumental architecture in the associated center. In the central and southwest valley (Joyce and Sheptak 1983) a consistent number of small structures was found to be associated with particular sizes of plazas. The great size of the CR-157 monumental architectural zone is larger than would be predicted based on the number of small structures at CR-157. The number of small structures in CR-157, CR-170, and CR-171 together is double that of the largest Late Classic sites studied, however, just as the monumental zone of CR-157 is double the size noted for the largest Late Classic sites.

Consequently, it appears that CR-157, CR-170, and CR-171 formed a single community in the Terminal Classic Period, one which was substantially larger than any previously known in the Ulua Valley. The internal organization of this community included three recognizable subdivisions. CR-170 and CR-171 have distinct civic-ceremonial compounds incorporating triadic arrangements of monumental structures on 50-meter-long plazas. These triads, opening east, may be oriented to the path of the sun. The significance of the east-west axis is supported by the unique cache of figurines from Group 1. Located east of the stone marker in the low central platform of this group was a pair of ceramic objects, both representing elaborately costumed males. West of the marker was a female figurine, simply dressed and carrying a two-handled pot. The east-west, male-female, ceremonial-secular contrasts embodied in this cache suggest that the axis of the sun's path had general significance for the community.

CR-157 displays a series of triadic groups, each opening south. As described for the Lowland Maya examples of this pattern (Ashmore

1986; 1989), these groups establish a north-south axis in which the northern, elevated locations are associated with the upperworld and ancestors, while the south is the secular, or underworld, direction. The ballcourt acts as a passage between the upper and under worlds (Gillespie 1985). The north-south orientation, in the Maya area, reflects greater concern with the ancestors of the elite and their claim to be able to transcend the divisions between the horizontal planes than with the east-west path of the sun.

The civic center of CR-157 may have served the population of the site as a whole. Its construction seems to reflect the labor of the entire population. To understand how that population might have been internally organized requires an analysis of the residential groups which formed its homesteads.

Households and Household Clusters

The small structures mapped at Cerro Palenque occurred as parts of 103 patio groups in 51 clusters, spatially segregated aggregations of patio groups (Ashmore 1981:47). Clusters were made up of from one to five patio groups; only 13 clusters had more than two patio groups. An estimate of the total area of each patio group was made by calculating the area of a polygon defined by the long axis of each group and the greatest measurement at right angles to the long axis. The modal dimensions of the patio group were found to be ca. 40 meters on a side, for an area of 1,600 square meters. The interior dimensions of the patio were ca. 15 meters on a side in 66 of 103 cases, with all but a few examples between 10 and 20 meters on a side.

The patio group has been compared to the household in contemporary Mesoamerica. Like contemporary Chorti households (Wisdom 1940:119−138), the patio groups at Cerro Palenque are made up of multiple structures and an associated formal open space. The structures in the patio groups, like those in Chorti households, fall into different size classes with distinctive features indicating different uses. The social group which occupied the Chorti household was a family, either nuclear or extended. As the family grew, the Chorti added more buildings. Eventually, adult children might break away and establish new households, initially smaller but growing in turn.

If the patio groups of Cerro Palenque represent the material remains of similar groups, then they would be expected to vary in size and number of structures as a reflection of similar developmental cycles. Such processes are indicated in the data from Copan (Leventhal 1983), where patio groups grow from an initial series of buildings by adding rooms and smaller buildings. Eventually, the patio groups at Copan can appear entirely enclosed by the aggregation of rooms. Interestingly, one structure in the patio group often is larger than the rest, is built with better-quality materials, and sometimes incorporates tombs. These "dominant structures" (Hendon 1987: 535–539) usually were established early in the developmental cycle and may be the residences of lineage heads (cf. Fash 1986b). The same pattern has been observed at the site of La Ceiba on the Sulaco River, where in each patio group, one structure is taller and larger than others, may show evidence for rebuilding and consequently must have been founded earlier than others in the group, and is a locus of burials (Benyo 1986 : 145–146, 251–253).

If patio groups at Cerro Palenque reflect the same processes, then the time-depth of development was much shallower than at Copan. None of the groups was completely closed off by accretion of new structures, the number of structures per group was low, and test excavations found little evidence of rebuilding. This agrees with the apparent short period of occupation suggested by the ceramic sequence.

The association of individual patio groups in clusters at Cerro Palenque provides further evidence that the time-depth of residential group development was relatively short. The individual patio groups were not randomly arranged. Rather, as mentioned above, they occurred in clusters of from one to five patio groups. The vast majority were either single-patio clusters (21 of 51 cases) or two-patio clusters (17 of 51 examples). If larger clusters usually represent the results of growth in individual households, accompanied by the establishment of new households, then the data from Cerro Palenque suggest that few households had developed beyond two generations.

The clusters were also examined for size regularities, like those identified for individual structures and patios. The attributes of clusters which were evaluated included the number of structures of the various size classes included and the approximate dimensions of the group as a whole, calculated in the same manner as described for individual patio groups. Tabulation of measurements of the 51 clusters showed peaks in the distribution, indicating modes for clusters of different sizes, in the intervals 500–899 square meters, 2,100–2,499 square meters, and 4,800–5,199 square meters (Figure 14). A parallel analysis (Joyce and Sheptak 1983) of dimensions of site features (large earthen platforms which supported groups of structures) reconstructed in an air photo survey of the disturbed settlement pattern of the central river valley (Sheptak 1982) identi-

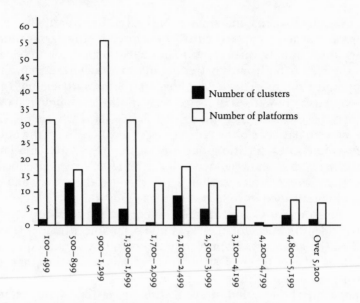

Figure 14. Size distribution of clusters at Cerro Palenque and platforms in central valley.

fied peaks at 900–1,299 square meters, 2,100–2,499 square meters, and 4,800–5,199 square meters, as well as a lower peak, at 100–499 square meters, not comparable to those identified in the clusters at Cerro Palenque (Figure 14).

The regularity of cluster sizes within the Cerro Palenque site zone suggests that clusters, like individual patio groups, represent some kind of social unit. Similar aggregation of patio groups is characteristic of Late Classic Lowland Maya sites, such as Copan (Leventhal 1979; Fash 1983a; 1983b; Hendon 1987). At the other extreme of Mesoamerican development, even the internal organization of cities such as Teotihuacan exhibits similar patterns (Millon 1974; 1981). Here, the clusters are replaced by apartment compounds in much closer proximity to each other. Yet these compounds have several of the features noted for Cerro Palenque and Copan. At least one major patio is present, with a temple or temples. The most prominent temple faces west. Groups of compounds form residential barrios comparable to the clusters of Cerro Palenque. Evidence for economic concentration by barrio is complemented by the presence in some barrios of larger, distinct temples presumed to serve the larger unit. Contemporary ethnography of Highland Maya communities suggests possible interpretations of the multiple-patio-group clusters of Cerro Palenque.

Among the Chorti of the Guatemala-Honduras border, individual compounds are organized in clusters composed of a chief household and one to eight dependent households. This "multiple household family" is linked by kinship ties, is localized, and is referred to by outsiders by a unique descriptive name (Wisdom 1940:246–249).

The Tzotzil of Zinacantan, Chiapas have settlement units comparable to these multiple household clusters, which have been labeled *sna*. While the individual household is composed of related individuals sharing a residential location, this larger group is not solely based on family ties. It includes from one to seven lineages, controls land tenure, and may jointly control ritual paraphernalia (Vogt 1969:127–130, 140–145).

The presence of units of settlement organization above the family compound in both areas is comparable to the existence of clusters at Cerro Palenque. The variation in the characteristics defining membership in these higher-order units suggests caution in extending a particular interpretation (such as that of extended families) to the Cerro Palenque clusters.

In the ethnographic examples, clusters are in turn part of larger settlement units, which in both cases are oriented to common water sources. The Zinacantec waterhole group (Vogt 1969:145–148) and the *valle* (*sian otot*, "many houses" in Chorti; Wisdom 1940: 216–220) unite groups of households which utilize common water sources. The Chorti clusters may be named for the stream they utilize. The waterhole group and *valle* are comparable in size. The waterhole group is made up of from 2 to 13 *snas*, which range in size from 4 to 40 houses (Vogt 1969:145). The Chorti *valle* is said to average 25 multiple household families, or 60 to 80 households (Wisdom 1940:220).

The Zinacantec settlement units are defined by common ritual. Each house compound has a house cross, located on a terrace outside the main dwelling. The *sna* has cross shrines also, including hilltop shrines dedicated to the ancestors and cave shrines dedicated to the Earth Lord, and a twice-yearly ceremonial circuit is made by the shamans of the *sna* to these shrines. The waterhole group also maintains cross shrines at the waterhole and on a hilltop, and a ceremonial circuit like that of each *sna* is made by the shamans of the waterhole group just prior to the smaller-scale ceremonies. Three distinct kinds of ceremonial linking the inhabitants of these domestic groups are involved: joint veneration of ancestors at all levels; prayers to the

Earth Lord by the land-holding unit; and prayers at the waterhole shrine by the waterhole group (Vogt 1969:128, 141–144, 147).

The waterhole group and Chorti *valle* are interesting potential analogues to the clusters at Cerro Palenque because they depend for their definition not on an archaeologically untested assumption of family relationships but on characteristics which can be detected in the archaeological record. Clustering, the first of these characteristics, has already been established. Orientation toward common water resources is not obvious in the archaeological case, but neither would it be by inspection alone in the case of Paste? (Vogt 1969:Map 7), where various waterhole groups have been mapped. The use of a particular water source is clearly not determined by proximity alone in this example. Most intriguing for the archaeological case is the provision of group shrines and the practice of group ritual documented for Zinacantan. Clusters at Cerro Palenque usually have at least one anomalous structure, and those tested in excavation were used in ritual, providing a potential analogue to the group shrines of contemporary Zinacantan.

The model suggested by the comparison of Cerro Palenque and the central Ulua Valley with modern Chorti and Zinacantec communities may be summarized. In both ethnographic cases, the individual residential compound (a combination of generalized living structures and smaller specialized function structures around a patio) is occupied by people who are members of a single family and their dependents. The household grows as the family grows, with adult children occasionally establishing independent residences nearby. Thus, compounds may be occupied by nuclear or extended families. The compound may correspond to the patio group at Cerro Palenque, which in turn is comparable to the two smallest platform size modes of the central Ulua Valley (100–499 square meters and 900–1,299 square meters).

Larger patio-group clusters at Cerro Palenque (with peaks at 2,100–2,499 and 4,800–5,199 square meters) may correspond to the Chorti multiple household families and Zinacantec *sna*. Both are groups of contiguous house compounds occupied by families farming adjacent lands. In Zinacantan, these groups practice common group rituals to the ancestors and Earth Lord.

The contemporary groups are in turn linked in larger clusters with common interests in water resources, practicing common rituals periodically at special group shrines dedicated to group ancestors and to the waterhole. In the Chorti area, the *valles* were the highest level of settlement organization. They may correspond to individual clusters of patio groups in both the central alluvium and Cerro Palenque zones which are sufficiently far apart to be identified as individual sites, such as CR-170 and CR-171.

While the Chorti *valle* is described as an individual settlement unit, the top level of organization in the area (Wisdom 1940), at Zinacantan similar units of organization (the waterhole groups) are part of larger social and political units. One or more waterhole groups may constitute a named hamlet (Vogt 1969:148–149). The hamlet is defined in relation to an over-arching community. Each hamlet elects representatives to the central government of this community and takes part in community-wide ceremonies. While the integrity of the hamlet is recognized in specific rituals, these differ from those of lower-level settlement units. The New Year and End of Year ceremonies involve a journey to the churches and sacred mountains near the community center, sacred sites common to all members of the community. This community is Zinacantan itself, united by periodic rituals and markets held in a specialized town center.

The subdivisions of Cerro Palenque which are marked by small plaza groups, CR-170, CR-171, and CR-157, may be compared to hamlets in modern Zinacantan. They are composed of a series of clusters of patio groups. At each of these levels—patio group, cluster, and plaza-group-focused site—evidence exists for the conduct of ritual, like that which in Zinacantec hamlets, waterhole groups, *snas*, and residences defines the social unit. The kinds of facilities available for ritual at the highest level, that of the plaza-group-focused sites, differ from those present at lower levels.

Cerro Palenque as a whole may be compared to the community of Zinacantan, with the large plaza group of CR-157 providing the facilities for the special services which bind the entire community together. In the central Ulua Valley, many platform clusters lack any evidence of monumental architecture and plazas, but at least four platform clusters did have such specialized facilities, among them the site of Travesía (Joyce and Sheptak 1983; Sheptak 1982:92–93; Joyce 1983). These groups of platform clusters with associated specialized architecture may in turn be compared to the community of Zinacantan and to the Cerro Palenque zone.

One implication of the ethnographic analogues is that beyond the level of the household, community development need not correspond solely to lines of kinship, but may respond to economic factors such as the exploitation of land and water. Another is that the most important features in defining a community may be the loci of group ritual on various levels, which serves to unify the members of residential units of different scales, and which leaves distinctive archaeological traces.

The archaeological site of Cerro Palenque represents the remains of a complex web of residential units and nonresidential zones. However, it was more than this. It was also the arena for day-to-day activities carried out by its population. While the nature of those activities is generally delimited by the identification of the different zones and structures within the site as residential, ritual, or public, there is much more concrete information available to identify activities carried out in the site. This information is provided by the distribution of artifacts among the different structures explored at the site.

The Site as an Activity Area

Excavations produced a large sample of ceramics, lithics, and, more rarely, other materials such as bone, shell, and seeds, stemming from distinct types of deposits. These artifacts and materials, and the contextual information provided by their associations with features and other artifacts, are the evidence to infer the kinds of activities carried out by the people of Cerro Palenque. The definition of artifact classes is the first step in this process.

Artifact Classification

Artifact analysis begins with the recording of attributes which are used to define classes of like materials. In order to study the use made of artifacts (and by extension, of the areas in which they were employed), the attributes recorded and the classes constructed must reflect the use of the artifact. Artifact form is one variable which is constrained by intended use. Most of the artifact classes defined at Cerro Palenque are based on form and reflect the use of the artifacts.

The procedure adopted to define artifact classes at Cerro Palenque was analytic rather than typological (Rouse 1960). Each artifact can be conceived of as resulting from a series of decisions between different possible forms or actions. For example, in constructing a ceramic vessel, the potter chose a general body shape and particular rim form and lip form. Each part of the artifact resulting from these individual decisions is a dimension of potential variation (Spaulding 1960). In analytic classification, each artifact is recorded as the values of each of the dimensions of variation. The value is an attribute of the artifact, and the artifact is fully described by its attributes.

Analysis of artifact records began with the tabulation of frequencies for each value recorded for each attribute. Inspection of the frequency histograms identified peaks, or common variants, and in the case of continuous attributes, such as rim diameter, intervals around peaks. The values of the attributes were redefined to reflect these peaks and intervals, and used as the basis for cross-tabulation. The cross-tabulation began with related attributes, such as those reflecting form. Cross-tabulations graphically depict clusters at intersections of specific values for each variable, illustrating not only the commonly repeated combinations but also the nature of variation around those combinations.

An example is the cross-tabulation of jar forms with tall necks and everted rims. Three different profiles were recorded for the necks of these jars: straight, out-flaring, and in-flaring. (These three profiles can also be represented as a section of a cylinder, a section of an inverted cone, and a section of a cone.) Cross-tabulation of these three neck profiles with rim diameter showed a regular relationship. The higher the rim diameter, the more outflaring the neck form. Cross-tabulation of the same attributes with others, such as surface treatment and paste, showed no other regular relationship. The differences recorded in neck profile were, accordingly, collapsed with the differences in rim diameter, to form three size categories of this vessel form.

Using these procedures, the attributes which distinguish between clusters of artifacts in the sample can be identified. The artifact classes defined are polythetic types (Bailey 1973). Each type is defined by the presence of a number of attributes drawn from dimensions of variation which are salient for that type. The number and kind of attributes required for assignment to a particular type may vary, and features which are critical to some types may be irrelevant to the definition of others. Polythetic artifact types were defined for ceramic vessels, ceramic artifacts, chipped and ground stone tools, and stone and shell ornaments.

Ceramic Vessels. The analysis of the 30,689 sherds (particularly 1,506 rim sherds) from Cerro Palenque identified 12 major vessel forms which combined with unique paste and surface treatment variants to form 19 classes of ceramic vessels (see Joyce 1985:239–329; 1987c:406–420 for details). These, in different combinations, made up the three ceramic complexes defined at Cerro Palenque: Late Classic (14 types), initial Terminal Classic (17 types), and late Terminal Classic (13 vessel types).

Two types of ceramic vessels were found only in Late Classic contexts. Unslipped grey bowls with flat bases and straight flaring walls were up to 7 centimeters deep. Other Late Classic vessels were open flaring-wall bowls made of a distinctive sandy pink paste, with a brushed surface and decoration in the form of geometric cut-outs, appliqué tabs, and appliqué finger-impressed bands. Similar vessel forms are usually called censers in the Maya area.

Six vessel types which began in the Late Classic continued in use into the initial Terminal Classic. Polychrome-painted, orange-slipped dishes, bowls, and cylinder vases were the most varied of these types (Figure 15). Simple round-sided bowls with rounded bases, brushed exterior, and orange-slipped interior were another of these types. Low dishes with ring bases, interior orange slip, and stamped exterior designs also survived from the Late Classic through the initial Terminal Classic. Finally, a common unslipped jar form of the Late Classic, with a round body, tall (over 6 centimeters), flaring neck, and pairs of strap handles, was also found in initial Terminal Classic deposits (Figure 16a–d).

In contrast, a core of six vessel types persists from the Late Classic through the end of the Terminal Classic. Changes in details of form, paste, surface treatment, and measurements were noted that distinguish early examples from late ones. More use of red slip, less use of incised motifs, and finer nonplastic inclusions are the most striking changes.

Collared jars were the single most common type of vessel in all of the ceramic complexes (Figure 16e–h). The typical round body terminates with a sharp out-turn marking one end of a low (1–3 cm tall), thick neck or collar. Some examples in the late Terminal Classic have round-section handles attached to the body. A minority of Terminal Classic examples also have a red-painted rim.

Basins are very deep (no complete forms were measured, but depths were over 10 cm), with vertical walls rising to a flattened rim (Figure 17a, b). The rim exterior is thickened to form a wedge. Basins may have two or four wide (4 cm) flat strap handles spaced around the exterior wall, attached below the thickened wedge rim. Both Late Classic and Terminal Classic basins may have red rim bands.

Flanged jars have a round body with a tall (to 20 cm), vertical neck (Figure 17c). The lip is rounded, and a narrow (1–2 cm) horizontal flange is located on the exterior neck within 2 centimeters of the lip. All examples had red paint on the exterior on the body and above the flange. In Late Classic examples, the unslipped exterior neck was incised in sets of horizontal parallel shallow wavy lines. None of the examples had handles.

Everted-rim jars have round bodies and a tall neck (over 8 cm high)

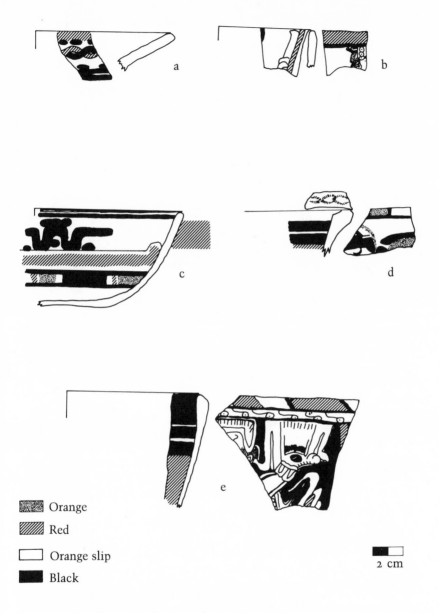

Orange

Red

Orange slip

Black

2 cm

Figure 15. Ulua Polychromes from CR-44: early (*a, b*); late (*c–e*); possible import (*e*).

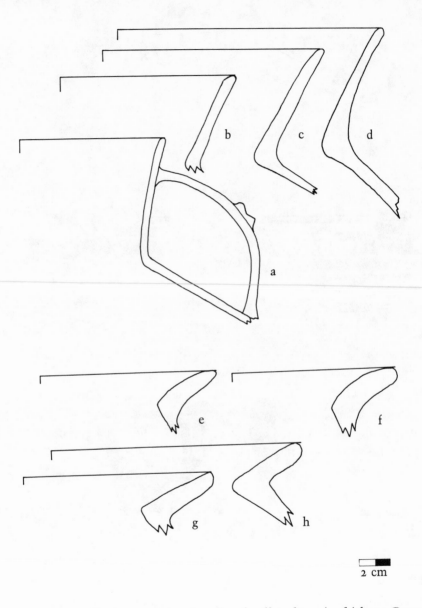

Figure 16. Flaring-neck jars (*a–d*) and collared jars (*e–h*) from Cerro Palenque. All Terminal Classic except *e* and *f*, Late Classic. All un-slipped except *c* and *d*, red-slipped.

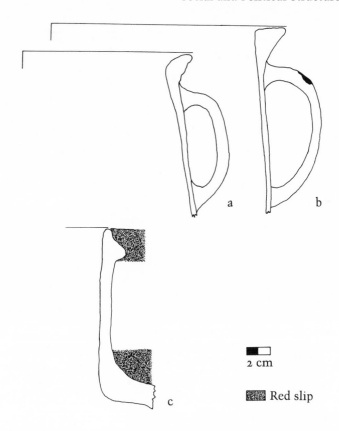

2 cm

▓ Red slip

Figure 17. Basins (*a, b*) and flanged jar (*c*) from Cerro Palenque.

which varies in profile from slightly in-flaring to out-flaring. At-tached to the neck is an out-turned rim (1–2 cm long), ranging from horizontal to a 45-degree angle. In some late Terminal Classic ex-amples, the everted rim is reinforced on the exterior, forming a slight wedge. Everted-rim jars have pairs of strap handles (1–2 cm wide) attached to the exterior neck below the everted rim. While both Late Classic and Terminal Classic examples are painted with red motifs and zones, the precise motifs and their placement differ. Late Classic examples have red motifs on a reserve ground on the body, surrounded by solid red (Figure 18). The neck may be un-slipped, with vertical incised multi-line motifs, or painted with red motifs. The rim interior also has red painted motifs. Terminal Clas-

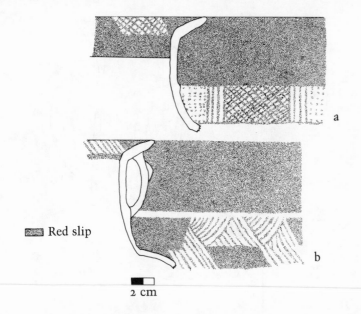

Red slip

2 cm

Figure 18. Late Classic red-painted jars from Travesía.

sic examples from Cerro Palenque entirely lack incised zones (Figure 19). In some examples, the exterior neck is left unslipped while the body, rim, and neck interior are solid red; this is especially common in examples with a wedge rim. Other examples have red geometric motifs on the exterior body, neck, and interior rim, with the neck invariably decorated with sets of horizontal wavy red lines.

Shallow plates (up to 3 cm deep, ca. 18 cm rim diameter) have no defined side wall, and are slightly convex (Figure 20a). Regular deep incised lines on the convex side form a checkerboard or diagonal lattice pattern. These plates have a characteristic square lip, and often preserve scars of some kind of handle arching above the concave side.

Braziers are tall "hourglass"-shaped vessels (a conical bowl supported on a conical pedestal), with three prongs slanting inward rising from the vessel lip. They are unslipped and roughly smoothed.

The unique characteristic of the Terminal Classic ceramic complexes is a new group of dishes, bowls, and vases, with distinctive forms, surface treatment and paste, labeled Tehuma Fine Buff (Figure 21). Along with the three Tehuma Fine Buff vessel types, new additions in the initial Terminal Classic complex are red-slipped flaring-wall bowls and an unusual spiked bowl.

Fine Buff dishes are shallow, wide vessels with low vertical walls

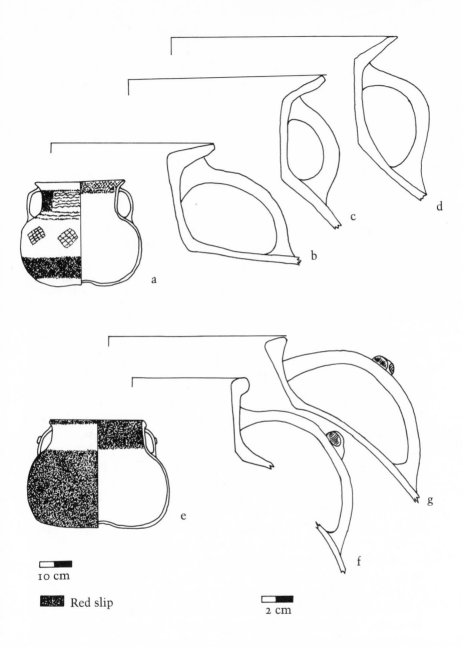

10 cm

Red slip

2 cm

Figure 19. Terminal Classic red-painted jars from Cerro Palenque:
early (*a–d*); late (*e–g*). Reconstruction of *d* (*a*) and of *f* (*e*).

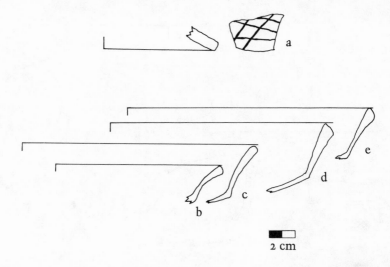

2 cm

Figure 20. Incised plate (*a*) and red interior-slipped flaring-wall bowls (*b–e*) from Cerro Palenque.

(1–3 cm high), flat interior bases, and three low feet. The diagnostic temperless paste varies in color from pink through orange to light yellow. Most sherds have a dark grey core. The surface, when it is well preserved, is burnished to a smooth matte finish but is unslipped. The interior base of these dishes is often incised with a series of roughly concentric circles superimposed on a cross, dividing the base into four quarters.

Fine Buff round-sided bowls have spherical bodies (5–8 cm deep) rising to a rounded rim or to a low, flaring neck. They rested on slightly flattened or dimpled bases. Their paste and surface treatment are identical to those described for Fine Buff dishes. The simple bowls have no further elaboration, but bowls with low necks often have an incised band at the juncture of the neck and body. This may be a single line or a geometric tress.

Fine Buff vases have a barrel-shaped or periform body supported by a flat base or low pedestal base. With paste and surface treatment like the Fine Buff dishes and bowls, vases have the most elaborate secondary surface treatment of this ware. Examples may have a single incised line below the rim on the exterior or pairs of incised lines below the rim and near the widest point of the body. Between these incised lines, some examples have incised geometric motifs and others have stamped designs difficult to reconstruct. Other Fine

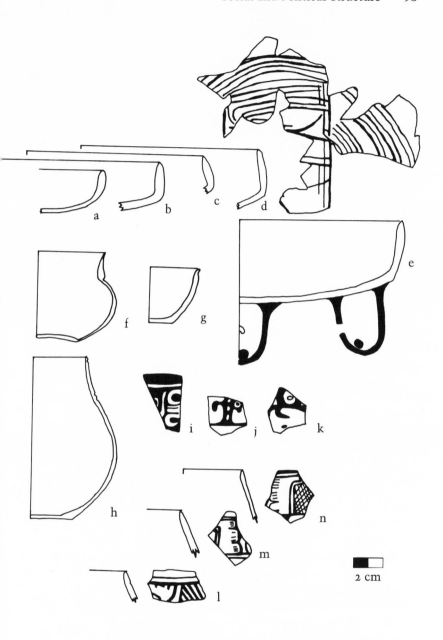

Figure 21. Fine Buff ceramics from CR-157: dishes (*a–e*), bowls (*f, g*), and vases (*h–n*).

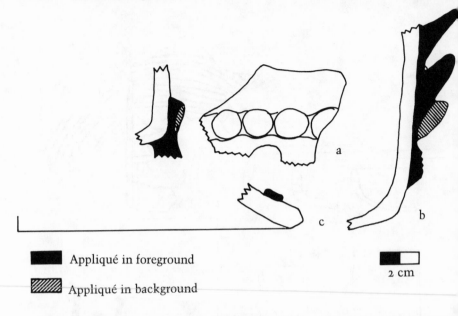

Appliqué in foreground

Appliqué in background

2 cm

Figure 22. Censers from Cerro Palenque: Late Classic (*a, c*) and Terminal Classic (*b*).

Buff vases have vertical grooves around the body below the widest point, a technique called "false gadrooning."

Flaring-wall bowls (Figure 20*b–e*) are wide and relatively shallow (4–7 cm deep). The interior base is flat, while the exterior base is slightly rounded. The exterior wall is slightly concave and flares out, and the rim is thickened. Only the interior walls are slipped; some interior base sherds show light grooving. Most examples are completely smudged, so that the exterior is black, the interior slip appears brown, and the paste is reddish-brown.

A new vessel form replaces the appliqué-decorated "censer" of the Late Classic. The paste used continues to be sandy, and the surface is smoothed and lightly brushed. The Terminal Classic examples, bowls with pedestal bases, have sets of appliqué spikes on their exterior wall, distinguishing them from Late Classic examples (Figure 22).

Although the majority of the vessel types typical of the late Terminal Classic were introduced in the initial Terminal Classic or even earlier, two types were found only in the latest complex. Tempered grey-slipped dishes are identical in form to Fine Buff examples, with low vertical walls, flat interior bases, and three low feet. They

are made of fine tempered paste, and covered on the interior and
exterior wall with a glossy, dark grey slip. Red-slipped, tempered-
paste round-sided bowls (5–8 cm deep) have curved walls rising to a
rounded rim. They are slipped on interior and exterior.

Other Ceramic Artifacts.   Other ceramic artifacts were rarer than
ceramic vessels. Most common were mold-made figurines and whistles (Figure 23). These were found in both Late Classic and Terminal
Classic contexts. All were representational, depicting human and
animal figures. The Late Classic examples came only from the test
pit in CR-44 and consisted of a small whistle shaped like a bird head
(Figure 23 e) and a figurine face with fat cheeks and an asymmetric
headdress with a profile bird image.

The Terminal Classic examples were more numerous, coming
both from trash deposits and, in the low central platform in Group 1,
from primary context. Only fragments of figurines were noted from
the trash deposits, some with a bird-head helmet also noted on one
figurine from the Group 1 cache. The two intact figurines from this
context depicted standing male and female figures. The male figure
wore a bird-head helmet and a feathered costume. In his hand was a
depiction of a conch shell trumpet, provided with a whistle mouth-
piece. The female figurine (Figure 23 a) was dressed in a skirt and
wore a square pendant on a cord around the neck. One hand was
raised, supporting an effigy of a two-handled jar resting on her head.
The cache also included the only example of an intact whistle from
the Terminal Classic site, depicting the head and shoulders of an
elaborately costumed human figure.

Two other types of ceramic artifacts of unknown function were
found only in Terminal Classic contexts: needle-shaped objects and
ovoid ceramic effigies (Figure 24). Needle-shaped objects, sometimes
described as pendants or limbs for composite figurines, are rods ca.
10 centimeters long with a pierced eye on one end. Since no bodies
for jointed figurines were found, that function seems unlikely. The
majority of examples were from trash concentrations; one was found
inside an ovoid effigy in Group 5 A.

Ovoid ceramic effigies are also of uncertain use. A molded and appliqué representation of a human or animal always marks the broad
end of the ovoid. The narrow end is open, and a slit runs from this
end along the top surface (with respect to the animal face). One
human-face ovoid was recovered in the initial Terminal Classic fill
in Group 6A. Other examples depicting a human face and a possible
fish were found in trash deposits in other groups. A unique pair were
recovered from the fill of the probable bench in the north structure

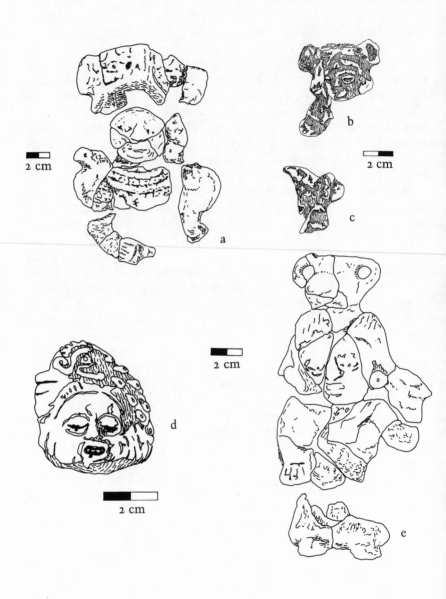

Figure 23. Figurines and whistles from Cerro Palenque. All Terminal Classic except *d*, Late Classic whistle. Figurines *a* and *e* from cache in Group 1.

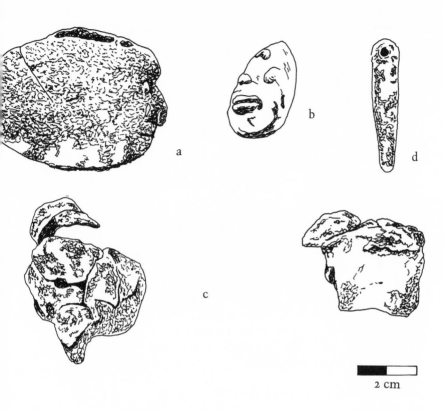

2 cm

Figure 24. Unusual ceramic artifacts from Cerro Palenque: ovoid effigies (*a–c*) and "needle" (*d*). Effigy *a* is from trash deposit in Group 5A; *c* is from cache in Group 4.

of Group 4. One represented a jaguar, with appliqué ears and snout. The other depicted a small bird from above, with the tail oriented down and the pointed beak oriented up. The details of the bird were also elaborated in appliqué.

Chipped Stone.   Material, dimensions, and form of the 992 chipped stone artifacts recovered were recorded. Formal categories represent different stages of the chipped stone industry (Sheets 1972), a blade tool industry using prepared polyhedral cores. Cores, large flakes, small flakes, polyhedral blades, and chunks from broken cores are the primary categories that represent this industry (Figure 25). Two general classes of materials were represented: obsidian (not available locally) and the abundant local cherts and quartzites.

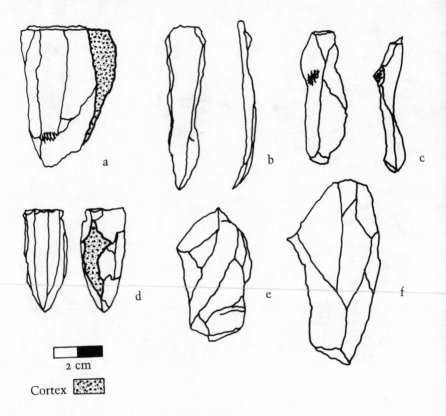

2 cm

Cortex

Figure 25. Cores (*a, d*), blades (*b, c*), and flakes (*e, f*) from Cerro Palenque. All local chert except *d*, obsidian.

Late Classic chipped stone included only blades and small flakes,
with obsidian predominant. Among the blades were a small number
made of green obsidian, presumably from the Pachuca source in
Mexico. Terminal Classic chipped stone was more varied. An abun-
dance of chert and quartzite cores, conical and 4–7 centimeters
long, accompanied the equally abundant chert and quartzite blades.
Distinctive from the Late Classic chipped stone is the presence of
large flakes and fragments of cores of the local cherts and quartzites.
Along with small flakes of the same materials, these items indicate
a Terminal Classic industry to produce polyhedral blade cores and
blades locally. Obsidian was less common, represented by a single
obsidian core (from a trash concentration in Group 3B), blades, and
small flakes.

Both obsidian and the local cherts were also used for other tools, bifaces and unifacial points-on-blades (Figure 26). The Late Classic sample included only a single obsidian biface, an eared form made of black obsidian. The Terminal Classic excavations included both obsidian and chert examples. All were ovate, and two obsidian examples had a short stem. Among the bifaces in the Terminal Classic site zone was a single ovate, stemmed example made of a fine-grained dark grey stone not locally available. In addition to the bifaces (presumably prepared from blanks manufactured from the initial large flakes struck from cores), a small number of obsidian polyhedral blades in Terminal Classic deposits were retouched unifacially to form small points.

Ground Stone Tools. Ground stone tools formed a major part of the material recovered as well. These 33 artifacts were grouped into general morphological categories, their dimensions recorded, and their material identified. Local basaltic lava was worked into metates, manos, mortars, and pestles. Metate fragments indicate the form was a rectangular, flat plate with three peg-shaped legs. The plate was ca. 4 centimeters thick, and curved on the lower edges. Manos were all cylindrical in cross-section, tapering from the center to squared ends. The two pestles identified were also cylindrical in section, but flared toward one end; one example was shaped like a golf tee. The single mortar recovered was a small-diameter basin with low walls. The Late Classic excavations yielded both mano and metate fragments; the larger sample from the Terminal Classic excavations included the other less common artifacts as well.

Other ground stone artifacts, all from Terminal Classic excavations, were made of finer-grained stones. Limestone was used to form a small ball and bar, found cached in a bench in Group 3A. A barkbeater of an unidentified extremely fine-grained dark grey stone, recovered in a trash deposit in Group 5A, was rectangular with a groove around the edges for hafting. One side was covered with coarse parallel grooves, while finer grooves marked the other side. A small celt of an unidentified very fine black stone was recovered in a trash deposit in Group 3B. Lens-shaped in cross-section, with a rectangular butt, the celt had heavy chipping on the bit indicative of use.

Stone, Shell, and Bone Ornaments. Unidentified fine greenstone ("jade"), another unidentified stone, marine shell, and dog and peccary teeth were employed in the Late Classic Period for small personal ornaments. In Group 2, two roughly spherical jade beads were

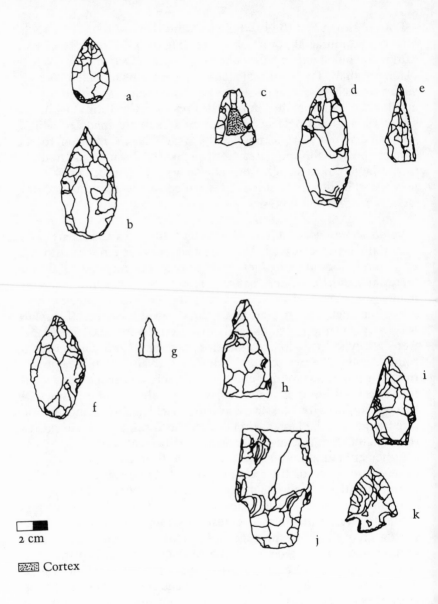

2 cm

▨▨▨ Cortex

Figure 26. Chipped stone tools from Cerro Palenque: bifaces (*a–f,* *h–k*) and unifacial point-on-blade (*g*). All Terminal Classic except *k,* from cache in Group 2. Chert (*a–e*); nonlocal grey stone (*f*); obsidian (*g–k*).

recovered, one intact in a cache, the second a half-bead from the surface on the southern structure. A third bead, a cylinder of an unidentified grey stone, was recovered from the patio floor in front of the western structure.

Other ornaments were recovered in the test pit at CR-44. These included a fragment of a greenstone "napkin ring" earspool and another jade bead. Two small marine shells, pierced as ornaments, included an *Olivella* "tinkler" and a bivalve (*Cardium?*). Both dog and peccary teeth pierced as ornaments were also included in this deposit.

Stone Sculpture. The final artifact category is stone sculpture. A large sample of carved stone pieces was recorded for CR-44, including examples removed from the site by previous investigators, examples located on the modern surface in survey, and examples excavated in Group 2. None of these pieces was found in situ, and the excavated examples clearly had formed part of upper architectural façades which had collapsed. The material of all the examples investigated is a rhyolite tuff (available on the western valley edge). Many of the pieces were too fragmentary to allow any description other than a characterization as geometric. Other pieces clearly represent three major themes.

An intact sculpture in a private collection and two fragmentary pieces excavated in Group 2 represent an anthropomorphic form. The stone is shaped in a series of three trapezoids, forming a silhouette like an inverted Christmas tree. The uppermost trapezoid has two round eyes, and sometimes a round mouth. The second trapezoid carries a rectangular panel with a tress motif, or a raised ring, occupying the position of a pectoral ornament. The final trapezoid has no carved features. These sculptures are most comparable to two examples excavated in the central zone of Travesía (Stone 1941:8).

A second group of sculpture fragments represented in excavation and survey consists of rectangular blocks with a series of raised rings like those forming the eyes on the most elaborate sculpture. At least one example has a raised rectangular band below the row of rings. Finally, a unique tenoned ring represents a schematic serpent head in profile. The eye is a pierced ring, and a knobbed ornament rises from the nose. The mouth is depicted as slightly open. Some other fragments of circular sculpture may have represented similar forms.

Only two examples of stone sculpture were recovered in the Terminal Classic site zone, both apparently of basalt. One was a freestanding plinth located out of context near an isolated structure on the northern edge of CR-157. One end of this sculpture was a rounded hemisphere. Below this hemisphere the column was squared, and a carved three-part molding ran around the four sides. The plain square column below this molding was broken irregularly. The other sculptured stone from the Terminal Classic site was a flat disk set in the west side of the ballcourt alley. This plain disk was placed at the juncture between the sloping and vertical walls of the flanking structure, on or near the alley center line. A similar disk was located in the equivalent position in an Early Postclassic ballcourt at Los Naranjos and, like the Cerro Palenque example, was not matched by a paired stone on the opposite side.

Artifact Function.   One further step is required in order to use artifact distributions to illuminate the different activities carried out at the site. This is the identification of the intended use, or function, of the artifact types defined. The major source of interpretation of artifact function is ethnographic analogy.

Specific ethnographic analogy is often based on an assumption of cultural continuity. For example, the use of Maya ceramic vessels is inferred from studies of modern Maya ceramic use (Reina and Hill 1978; R. H. Thompson 1958). More general ethnographic analogies may be drawn, based either on intrinsic properties of materials or on cross-cultural regularities. A pioneering study of contemporary Lenca potters (Castegnaro 1989) found a range of production techniques and vessel forms similar to those documented for Highland Maya potters (Reina and Hill 1978). The strongest similarities in technique and form are found in comparing eastern Guatemalan Chorti potters with the neighboring Lenca potters, suggesting that communication within the region spread ideas of form and specific techniques.

Cross-cultural study of the use made of ceramic vessels, intended to test hypotheses based on intrinsic properties of ceramics (Henrickson and McDonald 1983; M. F. Smith 1985), has established that the intended use of vessels places limits on their physical features. Four categories of use can be identified: storage, transport of liquids, cooking, and food-serving. Storage vessels often have lids, or a feature allowing a perishable lid to be attached. Vessels for transport of liquids often have restricted apertures and necks, and usually are provided with handles. Cooking vessels are usually thick walled and tempered to withstand fires. Most cooking vessels have wide apertures and walls. The presence of a griddle is typical of ceramic complexes in the New World. Ceramic food-serving vessels are generally open vessels, with finer paste and surface elaboration (such as painted or incised decoration). In contrast, storage, cooking, and transport vessels are more simply finished.

Using these observations, the general classes of vessels from Cerro Palenque can be ascribed tentative functions. Polychrome and Fine Buff dishes, bowls, and vases are the likely serving vessels in these ceramic complexes. Other rarer elaborate bowl types (e.g., orange-slipped and stamped, glossy black-slipped) may also be food-serving vessels. Based on their elaborate decoration, everted-rim jars may also be serving forms. Their tall necks, restricted apertures, and handles would suggest use to transport liquids.

Storage is the likely function of both collared jars and flanged jars. Most examples are not provided with handles. Both the flange and the thick collar would serve to fasten a perishable covering. Transport of liquids is the likely function of the Late Classic flaring-neck jars. The Terminal Classic ceramic complexes lack a significant number of comparable, unelaborated necked jar forms.

Basins and flaring-wall bowls are likely cooking forms, a conclusion reinforced by the uniform smudging of the Terminal Classic flaring-wall bowls. The scored plate, which shows evidence of fire-smudging, corresponds to the griddle form noted in other New World ceramic complexes. Distributional evidence discussed below suggests that these plates are associated with the three-prong braziers, together forming a kind of portable stove. This interpretation, distinct from the usual description of these braziers as "incensarios" of presumed ritual function, agrees with conclusions from distributional studies in the Sepulturas elite residential zones of Copan (Hendon 1987 : 352).

In addition to vessel forms corresponding to the classes recognized cross-culturally (Henrickson and McDonald 1983; M. F. Smith 1985), among contemporary Maya and Lenca (R. H. Thompson 1958 : 109; Reina and Hill 1978 : 27; Castegnaro 1989 : 28–29; Chapman 1985 : 103) specialized vessel forms used to burn copal incense are noted, bowls on a pedestal base with perforations for the escape of smoke. These correspond to unique vessel forms with appliqué decoration in both Late Classic and Terminal Classic complexes. The distinct distributional patterns of these censers, as discussed below, indicate that they were used primarily in ritual at Cerro Palenque.

The use of chipped stone tools cannot generally be inferred as easily from morphology, and no data on edge-wear exist to clarify the exact use made of stone tools at Cerro Palenque. In general, edge-wear analyses of chipped stone blades and bifaces in Mesoamerican sites testify to the all-purpose use of these tools for a wide range of cutting tasks (e.g., slicing, sawing, and scraping at Copan; Mallory 1984:241). Context of chipped stone tools at Cerro Palenque sometimes indicates nondomestic use, when they form part of caches. The use made of cores is clear, since they are the material for blade production. One special class of artifacts consists of the unifacially chipped points-on-blades. Similar small points are noted in Terminal Classic or later contexts from the Maya Lowlands, for example the Belize River Valley, Tikal, and Chichen Itza, where they are regarded as dart points (Willey et al. 1965:419–423).

The use of ground stone tools is generally inferred from their form. Manos and metates are the prime candidates for corn-grinding tools, although other materials may also have been ground on the same implements (Willey 1972:110–116; 1978:54–101). Mortars and pestles likewise were used in crushing or grinding food or other materials (such as clay, tempering material, or pigments). The single barkbeater recovered at Cerro Palenque represents a form universally believed to have been used in producing bark-paper or barkcloth (Willey 1978:54–101). The small celt, with indications of heavy wear, is one of the kinds of tools generally used for working wood or similar hard materials (Willey 1972:132).

The use of stone, bone, and shell ornaments as personal ornaments, and of stone sculpture to adorn buildings, is inherent in the definition of these types. More important may be their social function, a topic addressed in the next chapter. The activities most directly represented by these artifacts at Cerro Palenque, in any event, are disposal as refuse and, in a unique example, incorporation in a cache. In fact, the best evidence for the actual use of artifacts is their distribution in excavated contexts.

Artifact Contexts

The context of artifacts at Cerro Palenque includes the nature of the deposit and associated features. Most of the associated features at Cerro Palenque are architectural. As described previously, mounds representing small structures in patio groups can be divided on the basis of overall size and position in the patio group into four classes with modal basal dimensions of 25, 35, 50, and 100 square meters.

Excavated examples of the two larger classes included structures with built-in benches and others with large rectangular rooms defined by cobble wall bases. Structures with built-in benches had smaller floor space (ranging from 17 to 34 sq m). While none of these structures yielded trash deposits, they were a common site of caches.

The larger structures lacking benches (26 to 38 sq m) produced several of the trash deposits discussed below, but no caches.

The two smaller structure classes, with the majority of post-excavation dimensions under 10 square meters, included three distinct variants. Most elaborate were small relatively square rooms (under 1 m sq) with well-built walls. More common were rectangular structures with a single cobble wall base; two of the trash deposits were excavated from structures of this type. Finally, three of the small structures, located in the center of patios, were square platforms (ca. 3 m on a side) accompanied by caches.

Four kinds of deposits are represented in the excavations. Architectural fills incorporate artifacts which had been disposed of after use. They do not provide information on the primary use of the artifacts they contain. Small numbers of artifacts were recovered from the floors and terraces of patio groups and their buildings. While these artifacts were also refuse, they may be assumed to have been disposed of close to their use location. The six large trash deposits found in the Terminal Classic site are special cases: clearly, they are in a position at or near their original place of use. Finally, rare examples of artifacts in their primary context were recovered, most notably the many caches incorporated in the structures excavated.

Distinct patterns of caching are discussed below. Three contexts were noted: in three unique low central platforms; in the cobble fill in the northwest corner of three benches; and below the floor in the entryway to a room with a bench. Rare in situ deposits include single ceramic vessels on terraces adjacent to a room with bench in Group 1 and north of two small rooms in Group 3B.

A larger sample of artifacts came from six single-episode trash concentrations isolated in the Terminal Classic zone of the site. These were found in three kinds of locations. Trash concentrations in Groups 1, 3A, 3B, and 5 were found on the summit of the platform, on the off-patio side of a low cobble wall base. None of these structures had benches. Neither size nor architectural features of these structures were otherwise comparable. The summit area ranged from 38.5 square meters (Group 1) to 7 square meters (Group 3A), and structure plans included a single wall base (Group 5A), a single rectangular room (Group 3A), and a pair of rectangular rooms (Group 3B).

One unique trash concentration was contained within the western room of a structure in Group 5B, extending over the floor of the room and the surface of the bench. The final trash concentration was located in a corner formed by two stone walls marking the boundaries of the Group 3 cluster. A midden has been reported from a similar context at La Ceiba, southeast on the Sulaco River (Benyo 1986:91). Unlike the other trash concentrations at Cerro Palenque, this deposit cannot be associated with a single structure.

The distribution of artifacts within the site was evaluated by tabulating the frequency of each artifact class within each excavated patio group. Separate comparisons were made between the patio groups, different types of structures, and different types of deposits. If there were no differences between the groups, types of structures, and types of deposits, then artifact types should have frequencies representative of their overall frequency at the site and the proportion of the overall assemblage represented in any context. This was not the case, and the divergences in artifact distribution provide the evidence for interpreting the use made of different structures. They also provide evidence for evaluating the differential status of the households represented by the patio groups, a point considered in more detail in the next chapter.

The Distribution of Artifacts

The content of the six trash deposits excavated is summarized in Tables 2 and 3. The widest variety of materials was recovered from these deposits. Trash concentrations have very high proportions of large and medium collared jars and lower than expected frequencies of large everted-rim jars, flaring bowls, and medium round-sided bowls. The unique trash concentration inside the western room with bench in Group 5B contained many more collared jars than other trash deposits, but no small or medium dishes, and only small hemispherical bowls.

All trash deposits included material from the core-blade industry based on local cherts and quartzites (Table 2). Chert blades and flakes were found in every trash deposit, and chert cores were recovered from the majority. Obsidian blades and flakes were present in most trash deposits, and one obsidian core was recovered, in the trash deposit in Group 3B. Other chipped stone artifacts were found rarely in trash deposits: a single biface in each of three locations and a unifacial point-on-blade in a fourth deposit.

Grinding tools (manos, metates, and pestles) were part of three of the trash deposits. This included an intact mano, from the unique trash deposit inside a room in Group 5B. Finally, the only examples of a celt and a barkbeater were from individual trash deposits.

In general, trash deposits contained a high proportion of jars, compared to other kinds of deposits, and the greatest diversity of lithic remains. Unique materials were also found in trash deposits. Ex-

Table 2. *Distribution of lithics in trash deposits*

| | Group and Patio | | | | | |
Artifact Type	1	3B	3A	3A/B[a]	5A	5B
Obsidian blades	6	10	3	6		2
Obsidian flakes	5	3	2	5		2
Chert blades	4	8	1	3	11	10
Chert flakes	47	22	14	7	42	39
Chert cores	6	1			1	5
Obsidian core		1				
Grinding tools	3			2		1
Bifaces	1	1				1
Unifacial point-on-blade			1			
Small celt			1			
Barkbeater						1

[a] Corner between 3A and 3B.

amples of the ceramic ovoid effigy were found in two of these contexts, in one case accompanied by a ceramic needle-shaped object. The least common material in these contexts, as in the site in general, was organic remains. Nonetheless, one deposit included burned beans (Group 5A), while another yielded corozo palm nut husks (Group 3, against the cluster boundary walls).

Caches, in contrast, contained a very restricted range of materials, primarily lithics and ceramic artifacts. They entirely lacked ceramic vessels. Caches in benches included a single, unused basalt mano; a limestone ball and bar; and three ceramic artifacts and a chert biface. Caches in central platforms included a single obsidian blade and pebbles; a stemmed obsidian biface; a *Spondylus* shell containing a single, globular jade bead; three ceramic artifacts (a female figurine, a male figurine, and a whistle); and a chert biface. The cache in the entryway of a room with bench contained three chipped stone bifaces, two obsidian and one chert. Caches are most distinctive in the high number of bifaces and ceramic artifacts which they contain, the majority of the samples from the site of these artifact classes.

The distribution of artifacts in different kinds of contexts alone is not as informative as the way that these distributions vary with associated features. The most significant kinds of features identified at Cerro Palenque are types of buildings. Five distinct groups of structures with different profiles of associated artifacts (using for this purpose all artifacts not included in construction fill) can be defined.

Structures with built-in benches are the most distinctive architectural form. They are loci for caches and with one exception do not have associated trash deposits. Low central platforms, although varied in precise features, are remarkably regular in size (9 sq m), and are exclusively sites of caches.

The majority of the remaining structures had low cobble walls, undoubtedly the bases of perishable buildings, defining roughly rectangular or square rooms. These structures were varied in size and precise details. Two trash concentrations were associated with larger examples (falling in the 50-square-meter structure size class) and a third trash concentration was associated with one of the smaller examples.

Among the numerous smaller structures, two plans stand out. Buildings with rectangular summit areas marked by a single cobble wall base suggest partially open lean-to structures. One trash concentration was associated with a building with this plan. In contrast, some structures have rooms with well-defined walls outlining spaces of 1 square meter or less. These small rooms might better be characterized as bins.

Table 3 summarizes the frequencies of ceramic vessel types in five classes of excavated buildings. Structures with trash concentrations are grouped together for this purpose, since the presence of trash concentrations in these localities provides a sample differing markedly from the general refuse more commonly present. The remaining structures are divided into four classes: structures with benches, large and small structures with simple cobble wall bases (ancillary structures), and nondomestic (ritual) structures. The latter category groups together the low central platforms, the anomalous "group temple" from Group 2, and the isolated northern structure in CR-157. These structures are united by the presence of particular ceramic vessel types not found elsewhere.

Structures with benches have high proportions of small dishes and large elaborate jars, forms presumably associated with serving of food. Although the sample size is small, structures with benches also account for the majority of braziers and plates. Ancillary structures contrast sharply, with no large everted-rim jars or basins. Ancillary structures have high numbers of large collared jars, and the entire sample of flanged jars. The latter two forms, lacking handles and ranging up to 50-centimeter rim diameters, are apparent long-term storage vessels. Nondomestic (ritual) structures have large numbers of basins and medium and large elaborate jars. The presence of elaborate jars in nondomestic structures and structures with

Table 3. *Distribution of ceramic vessel forms by architectural units*

		Structure Types				
Vessel Form (Number of Rims)		With Bench[a] (N = 7)	With Trash[b] (N = 6)	Ancillary Large[c] (N = 7)	Small[d] (N = 3)	Ritual[e] (N = 5)
Dish	(76)					
Small	(24)	13	5	3	2	1
Medium	(37)	8	21	6	1	1
Large	(15)	6	5	3	1	0
Basin	(26)	6	11	0	0	9
Round-sided bowl	(222)					
Small	(86)	29	36	14	2	5
Medium	(136)	46	34	33	3	20
Flaring-wall bowl	(39)	16	7	9	1	6
Everted-rim jar	(140)					
Small	(77)	27	30	13	3	4
Medium	(51)	8	19	13	1	10
Large	(12)	9	1	0	0	2
Collared jar	(105)					
Small	(46)	15	18	9	1	3
Medium	(48)	11	22	11	1	3
Large	(11)	0	10	1	0	0
Flanged jar	(5)	0	0	3	2	0
Totals	(613)	194	219	118	18	64
Rims per structure		27.7	36.5	16.9	6	12.8

[a]All structures with benches, plus east structure of Group 6B.
[b]All structures with trash concentrations.
[c]Structures without bench or trash, having defined wall bases for rooms over 1 square meter.
[d]Structures with rooms of 1 square meter or less.
[e]All central platforms, plus one isolated structure with figural censer and sculpture.

benches is striking. Ritual structures and benches have other notable commonalities: only these locations yielded caches, and all the censers (although too uncommon to include in the table) stemmed from ritual structures or rooms with benches.

The distribution of lithics (Table 4) further confirms the separation between these kinds of structures. Structures with benches had no bifaces (except in a cache), while grinding stones were not uncommon. The full range of chert lithic debris—cores, flakes, blades,

Table 4. *Lithics across structure types*[a]

	Structure Class		
Artifact Type	With Bench (N = 7)	Ancillary (N = 10)	Ritual (N = 5)
Obsidian blades	20	0	9
Obsidian flakes	11	0	0
Chert blades	40	23	7
Chert flakes	137	133	30
Chert cores	21	20	0
Obsidian core	0	0	0
Grinding tools	8	5	4
Bifaces	0	2	1
Unifacial obsidian point-on-blade	1	0	0

[a]Based on all material except fill and caches (which do not reflect activities carried out at the location).

and chunks derived from shattered cores—is found with these structures, indicating core-blade production. An obsidian unifacial point-on-blade was associated with a structure with a bench in Group 6A. Nondomestic structures include deliberately cached lithics, but also obsidian and chert blades and flakes, and in two cases (Group 1 and Group 6A) manos. The absence of cores is notable and suggests that the other lithics were deposited through use, not as a result of manufacture.

Grinding stones were found in four ancillary structures, accompanied by chert blades, flakes, and cores, suggesting a multipurpose work area. Chert knapping, suggested by chert cores, flakes, blades, and chunks, was associated with seven ancillary structures. The only bifaces noted outside trash deposits or caches were chert bifaces from terraces adjacent to very small, well-built rooms. The same two locations yielded the entire sample of flanged jars at the site.

In summary, artifact distributions confirm the architectural differences noted and testify to distinctive activities associated with different structures. Food serving and consumption, chert knapping, and ritual are all attested for structures with benches. Nondomestic structures provided evidence for food preparation (grinding), serving and consumption, ritual, and some tasks involving the use of blades and flakes. Most ancillary structures provide evidence of chert knapping, and about half of these structures provide evidence of grinding. Only storage is suggested by the ceramics associated with these locations, except in the rare cases of trash deposits. Storage is strongly suggested by the presence of very large, handleless jars adjacent to very small rooms, locations which also produced the only general utility tools (bifaces) not in caches.

Comparisons between entire patio groups produced fewer contrasts, as would be expected if the patio groups represent comparable social groups. One notable exception to this generalization, returned to in the next chapter, is the proportions of locally available and exotic lithic materials. While blades are present throughout the site, the proportion of obsidian to chert varied greatly (Table 5). Other less abundant exotic materials also were found primarily in groups with high proportions of obsidian, such as Group 1.

The most important implication of this finding is that different attributes of the same artifacts may reflect the effects of distinct processes. Formal attributes are related to the use of artifacts. Based on formal attributes, while different kinds of buildings were the sites of different activities, each patio group produced evidence of the full range of activities. Other attributes, such as material, reflect differential access to resources, or wealth, among the apparently functionally equivalent patio groups.

Table 5. *Proportions of exotic chipped stone by group*

Group	% Obsidian Blades		% Exotic Bifaces
CR-44	90.8		50
	4.1	green obsidian	—
Test pits	89		100
	0.6	green obsidian	—
Group 2	93		100
	8.4	green obsidian	—
CR-157	33.6		44
Group 1	51.06		100
Group 3A	45.2		—
Group 3B	29.8		50
Group 3 total	31.3		50
Groups 5A and 5B	20.3		40
Groups 6A and 6B	32		0

Activities of the Community at Cerro Palenque

The evidence reviewed above provides a basis to describe the activities carried out by the population of Cerro Palenque. These activities include subsistence production, storage, food preparation, food serving and consumption, ritual, and lithic production.

Unmodified organic materials, recovered primarily from architectural fill, provide a glimpse of the subsistence base of Cerro Palenque. Other evidence for subsistence activities is provided by the manos and metates, grinding stones generally associated with corn processing. No direct evidence of corn agriculture was recovered, but a sample of burned beans, part of the maize-beans-squash agricultural pattern, was recovered in a trash deposit in Group 5A.

The direct evidence for subsistence attests to a varied exploitation of both plant and animal resources. Coyol palm seeds, a wild resource available in the hill zone, would have provided protein and oil. Riverine snail shells (*jutes*), crab claws, clam shells, and turtle shell plates testify to the extensive use of the neighboring river as a source of protein. Deer bone and peccary teeth are evidence for hunting, perhaps within the hill zone.

A specialized form of structure with unusual artifactual remains is probably some kind of storage facility. The rooms in these structures are very small (1 sq m or less), but have well-constructed stone walls and floors. In two cases, associated terraces yielded both biface fragments and sherds of an unusual large handleless jar form. The great size (50-cm rim diameter) and lack of handles make clear that these jars were not portable, and use as storage jars seems indicated.

Food preparation is identifiable based on the several trash concentrations recovered at Cerro Palenque. These include a distinctively high proportion of plain jars with pronounced collars, a probable general utility form used for storage and transport of materials. No other loci yielded the high proportions of this vessel form. An indication that these trash deposits represent a food-preparation area, not simply storage, is provided by the great diversity of other associated materials. Ceramics include serving vessel forms: bowls, dishes, and elaborate jars. Lithics include both chipped and ground stone tools. Chipped stone bifaces from these deposits are considered to be general utility tools. Ground stone pestles and manos from these deposits provide direct evidence of food processing, an inference further strengthened by the recovery of beans and coyol husks from two separate trash deposits. Finally, the single trash deposit found inside a room was associated with a burned circle of clay, a possible sign of the use of a ceramic brazier.

The primary indication of food serving and consumption is relatively high proportions of serving vessel forms, bowls, dishes, and tall-necked jars with elaborate decoration whose tall necks, pairs of handles, and size suggest use in transporting liquids. These were most strongly associated with structures with benches. Other evidence for food serving and consumption at the same locations is the presence of braziers, plates, and the burned circular patches which mark the use of these portable stoves. The plastered terrace adjoining the bench in the south structure of Group 2 is an example. Fragments of a three-prong brazier were part of the general lots from this structure, and the plaster appeared to be burned.

While food preparation and serving were the primary activities indicated for structures with benches, both ritual and production of chipped stone lithics were also associated with these multipurpose structures. Neither activity was solely associated with structures with benches, a circumstance which allows a fuller exploration of these activities.

Lithic working debris littered terraces on structures with built-in benches. The evidence for the local core-blade industry is the occurrence of the full range of chert material, from prepared polyhedral cores, debitage, and flakes through blades and chunks from broken cores. The full range of chert working remains was also found on low platforms supporting at most a single row of cobbles, the base for a perishable wall, with few other artifacts. These platforms may have served as locations for other manufacturing activities whose evidence was perishable.

The final activity represented in the general household group is ritual. Ritual activities are represented within the site in the great plaza of CR-157, in the isolated northern structure of CR-157, and in individual residential groups. The evidence for ritual is complex, consisting of unusual artifacts, materials, and features; the symbolic content of these materials; and the behavior represented by the distributions of artifacts in locations of ritual practice.

The primary feature indicating ritual behavior is the cache. Caches incorporate a limited range of artifacts and are found in a limited range of locations. Caches were located only in benches and in low central platforms. They included only lithics, ceramic artifacts, greenstone, and exotic shell.

The suggestion that caching marks central platforms and structures with benches as locations of ritual activity is supported by the distribution of ceramic censers with appliqué decoration. These vessels are found in low central platforms and structures with benches; in the unique "temple" on the east side of Group 2; and at CR-157, in the main plaza, ballcourt, and isolated northern structure.

The ceramic artifacts included in caches are representational, and suggest some of the symbolism underlying ritual behavior at Cerro Palenque, a point discussed in detail in a later chapter. Figurines include a human figure dressed in a feathered bird costume. A feathered costume is also featured on a human effigy censer at the isolated northern structure of CR-157. Ceramic effigies of a bird and a jaguar reinforce the importance of the bird theme and add to it the common Mesoamerican concern with the jaguar. The choice of a jade bead and thorny oyster shell for the Late Classic cache may also reflect widespread Mesoamerican symbolism. More generally, the cached artifacts imply that certain kinds of behavior were involved in ritual at the site.

Ritual behavior may have included preparation and serving of food, especially drink; blood sacrifice; and costumed dance. In addition to caches, low central platforms yielded high proportions of ceramic serving vessels, especially the elaborately decorated handled jars. Grinding stones were also among the artifacts recovered in these areas. These artifacts hint that the rituals practiced in these locations included feasting, or at least drinking, as is common today throughout Latin America (see Wonderley 1988 for a similar interpretation of remains at Late Preclassic Río Pelo).

The inclusion of chipped stone bifaces in caches suggests the possibility of ritual bloodletting, a practice with widespread currency in Mesoamerica (Schele and Miller 1986; Joyce et al. 1986; Klein 1987). In the Lowland Maya area, cached chipped stone forms have been found to lack use-wear, and in at least one instance, evidence of human blood was recovered from such pristine lithics (Dr. Eleanor Downes, personal communication, 1987). The strongest argument for this interpretation of cached lithics at Cerro Palenque can be made in the case of the central platform in Group 2, whose founding cache contained a single, entire obsidian blade.

Artifact distributions for low central platforms indicate that significant numbers of blades were recovered, although none of the material representing blade production was found. This further suggests that ongoing ritual at these locations included blood sacrifice.

Finally, the depiction in figurines and censers of humans in feathered costumes suggests the possibility that masked dancers participated in ritual. While this is necessarily speculation, such masked dances could have employed ceramic musical instruments like the whistle in the cache in Group 1 (cf. Healy 1988).

The picture that emerges from this discussion of evidence for behavior at Cerro Palenque is one of a wide range of activities centered in independent residential compounds. Within the compounds, specialized structures existed for uses such as storage, lithic production, and cooking. A unique class of structures were sites of ritual. However, the individual group was dominated by a multipurpose structure with evidence for many of these specialized tasks.

The individual residential groups were clustered into larger units, comparable to those noted as intermediary levels of community organization in contemporary Maya communities. Variation between groups and clusters was not marked. However, evidence for activities in the residential groups diverges strikingly from that for plaza areas with monumental architecture. The suite of residential groups and clusters associated with monumental architecture and plazas defines the community of Cerro Palenque.

In the Late Classic this community was limited to the hilltop groups. In the Terminal Classic Period, the community grew. Its integration was centered on CR-157 with its great plaza and ballcourt complex. The site was large enough to support at least two discernible subsidiary foci of public activities as well, CR-170 and CR-171.

As a single community, Cerro Palenque occupied a place in the sociopolitical system represented in the Ulua Valley which is also subject to interpretation. The political organization of the site is the topic of the final section of this chapter.

Political Structure: The Site as a Center

Variation within the site zone of Cerro Palenque was sufficiently great to allow the identification of distinct size classes of structures and the open space, patios and plazas, with which they were associated. The discussion of social structure and behavior has exploited the evidence provided by the small patio groups. An interpretation of the political structure of the site and the region depends on the interpretation of the larger plaza groups, both as markers for distinct levels of community and as sites for a suite of activities.

For this purpose, the variation within the site zone is too limited to be useful. Cerro Palenque must be considered against a background of comparable, independent sites. The data from the Proyecto Arqueológico Sula provide abundant examples of sites with the same kinds of features, many of which are dated at least approximately as Late Classic contemporaries of the initial settlement at Cerro Palenque. A series of analyses (Joyce and Sheptak 1983; Joyce 1987b; Pope 1985; 1987; Robinson 1982; 1983; 1986; 1989; Sheptak 1982) have defined the features of a series of distinctive site types.

In these analyses, the existence of plaza groups with monumental architecture has been identified as a key marker of a small number of the 500 sites identified in the Ulua Valley. Monumental structures are buildings which are, even in their collapsed form, over 2.5 meters tall and measure from 10 to 30 meters on a side. They occur in groups around large, open plazas, spaces 50 meters or more on a side.

Since plazas with monumental architecture include the facilities assumed to have public, civic, and religious functions, the sites with these facilities form a special class. These may be called centers, a reference to their function as a center for specialized activities (Willey 1981 : 391–394). Cerro Palenque was, from its earliest phase, a center.

Site Hierarchy and Regional Organization

Analyses of large samples of centers from the Ulua Valley (Joyce and Sheptak 1983; Robinson 1986) have compared the features of these sites. Among the variable features are the size of the plazas, number and size of monumental structures around the plaza, and number of other structures or patio groups in the sites. Both analyses identified regular patterns defining large and small centers.

Small centers have plazas ca. 50 meters on a side and up to 80 structures overall. Late Classic Cerro Palenque, CR-44, was a small center. Large centers have plazas over 100 meters on a side, and up to 250 structures. The settlement pattern of the Late Classic Ulua Valley is characterized overall by a number of equally large and complex centers. Terminal Classic Cerro Palenque is a unique large center, with a plaza twice the size of any other known from the Ulua Valley, and twice as many structures in total, reaching its peak in apparent isolation.

If the two size classes of centers are assumed to be part of a functional hierarchy (Johnson 1977), then at least three levels of sites characterized the sociopolitical system of the Late Classic Ulua Valley. Spatial analyses showed that large centers are evenly spaced on both eastern and western sides of the valley (Joyce and Sheptak 1983; Robinson 1983; 1986). Small centers are distributed within the local area defined around the evenly spaced large centers, suggesting dependence on the larger centers. The lowest level of the site hierarchy, sites without plaza groups, may be subdivided into a number of categories based on the nature and number of small structures they contain and the formality of their organization (Robinson 1986). However, the lack of distinctive public facilities suggests these are all residential sites. The overall conclusion is that the political system represented had three levels: residential hamlets, small villages, and larger towns.

A number of independent, three-level polities can be defined for the Ulua Valley. On the extreme southeast, Robinson (1982; 1983; 1989) has described the Late Classic settlement organization centered on the site of La Guacamaya. She demonstrates that La Guacamaya appears to have been the earliest established of the centers in the area. Small centers developed as part of the filling-in process around the initial center. Robinson indicates that architectural features within the main center are stylistically related to the subsidiary centers and speculates that they may represent the integration of these small centers in the polity based at La Guacamaya. Her analysis indicates that control of agricultural land may have been a factor in the integration of the southeast polity.

Late Classic Travesía, now largely destroyed, appears to have been the center of a similar polity located in the central alluvium along the Ulua River (Joyce and Sheptak 1983). Other major centers, such as Curruste (Hasemann, Van Gerpen, and Veliz 1977), which are equivalent in scale to La Guacamaya and Travesía, are candidates for the centers of similar, less well documented, settlements. Decorated serving vessels from Curruste and Travesía present clear contrasts, perhaps indicating that these centers maintained distinctive traditions of material culture (Sheptak 1987a; Joyce 1987b).

These large centers appear to be independent, contrasting in specifics of site organization, public architecture, and artifacts. They appear to represent the material remains of independent, potentially competing polities. Each incorporates plaza groups with monumental architecture, including ballcourts at Travesía and La Guacamaya. Distinctive stone sculptures were included at La Guacamaya, Travesía, and Curruste. These features suggest that the process of political integration was based partly on common public ceremonies which took place in these public zones.

Late Classic Cerro Palenque, with its small size and relatively simple public zone, appears to have been a subsidiary of a polity centered elsewhere in the valley, perhaps at Travesía. In the Terminal

Classic, Cerro Palenque became a unique example of the large center, incorporating within itself two small centers, reaching a size unprecedented in the valley. In the following chapters, the implications of this interpretation for social dynamics at Cerro Palenque are addressed.

Chapter 5. Social Dynamics: Interaction

IN THE last chapter, the data from Cerro Palenque were used to reconstruct the kinds of enduring units of social and political structure that an anthropologist might have identified in the living community. Some examples of behavior which could be inferred from the data were also discussed. Necessarily, this discussion presented a static picture of the site as if observed at a single point in time.

In order to make sense of Cerro Palenque, however, the dynamics of the development of the community and its transformation through time need to be explored, a task that will occupy the next two chapters.

Social Interaction: A Model

I rely on an explicit model of social dynamics emphasizing the way social power is developed and exercised (Adams 1975). The central concept in this model is social power, defined somewhat differently than is usual in anthropological studies (ibid.: 9–20). Social power, rather than being conceived of as some kind of objective commodity, is based on the perceptions of actors joined in a relationship (ibid.: 19–20). This shift in emphasis acknowledges the fact that human beings act, not on the basis of an objective assessment of the state of the world, but on their perception of this condition. Perception limits and channels the understandings on which human actors base their decisions and actions.

The kind of relationships central to this model are those in which actors are joined by their mutual interest in an object or goal (Adams 1975: 9–10, 106–109). If one actor is perceived to have greater influence or control over the object or goal, then that actor will stand in a position of power over the other actors in the relationship (ibid.: 13–14). The more powerful actor will be able to influence the behavior of the less powerful due to their common interest and shared belief in the greater control of the more powerful actor (ibid.: 121).

The choices which actors make are held to be limited by the goals or objects addressed and the perceived relationships of power which surround these goals. While this model clearly does not encompass all behavior, it is particularly useful for an exploration of sociopolitical and socioeconomic interactions.

The actors in social interaction may be individuals or groups of people. Adams (1975:52–67) uses the term "operating unit" for groups of actors oriented toward a common goal in some relationship of power, and distinguishes operating units in which there exists "an identification of commonality, with the consequent change in behavior of individual [operating] units to use this fact to their own advantage" (ibid.:55). Such identity groups can be constituted variously, through the use within the group of some common criteria of identification (ibid.:58). When the perceived common identity becomes the basis for concerted action, the identity unit becomes a coordinated unit (ibid.:60). These "form the major basis for the emergence of more highly centralized units" (ibid.).

Kinship groups, such as the family, lineage, or clan, may be operating units. Ethnic groups are another example. The advantage of the general terminology is clear when applied to certain parts of the population of Cerro Palenque. For example, the inhabitants of a patio group, presumed to be a co-residential unit perhaps based on kinship, can be studied as an identity group, while leaving open the issue of the basis of self-identification. As a group, the inhabitants would have had common goals toward which they were directed. The inhabitants of a patio-group cluster, suggested analogues of the Zinacantec waterhole group and Chorti *valle,* may have been related through kinship, co-residence, or other identification. The use of the term "operating unit" assumes only the common orientation of these inhabitants in some set of activities; the label "identity unit" further implies the assumption that the inhabitants recognized their common interest and identity.

Adams (1975:208–217) identifies two main dynamic processes in interactions of social power. These he calls centralization and coordination. Centralization results from the formation of asymmetric relations of power. As actors acknowledge that another party or group has control over an object or goal of mutual interest, they enter into asymmetric, vertical links (ibid.:74–75). Their actions are directed upward toward the party in a position of power. Such relationships are hierarchical, as each actor or group in turn is involved in further relationships with other parties.

The complementary process is coordination, the formation of horizontal links between operating units (Adams 1975 : 76–77). Coordination results when two actors or groups, recognizing a common identity and a mutual goal, perceive neither party as in greater control of that goal or object (ibid.: 57, 210).

The intersection of these two processes accounts for social dynamics, both the progressive evolution of levels of integration and oscillation between centralized and coordinate units (Adams 1975 : 212–213, 217–278, 285–298). In order to apply this model to Cerro Palenque, I first identified evidence for the existence of operating units at the site. I then was able to suggest the existence of centralized, hierarchical relationships and horizontal, coordinated relationships maintained by these operating units.

Operating Units at Cerro Palenque

I assume that co-residents in groups constituted an operating unit sharing certain activities, including ritual. The inhabitants of each level of the community outlined in the previous chapter would have acted as an operating unit and may have constituted an identity group. The co-residents of the patio group are the lowest-level unit at the site. Together, the inhabitants of patio groups forming a cluster might have formed a second group. The populations of CR-44, CR-170, and CR-171, carrying out common ritual in the plazas of these small centers, might be other distinct operating units. If the inference from spatial analysis that small centers are subordinate to a single large center is correct, then the inhabitants of the Terminal Classic polity centered on CR-157 and those of the polity of which Late Classic CR-44 was a part would be higher-level operating units. Finally, we can investigate the possibility that these polities, the highest-order units of settlement in the valley, would be part of a higher-order operating unit. The identification of operating units at these different levels is based on the evidence of shared goals and activities. In order to interpret these operating units as identity groups, it would be desirable to identify material evidence of an asserted group identity, and a possible common goal or object around which these units would have organized, for each level.

The co-residents of the patio group are the fundamental operating unit of the proposed social system of Cerro Palenque. The diversity of activities represented in each group supports the identification of the patio group as a household. The common goal of the household is economic and social survival. Food preparation, storage, and consumption, stone tool production, and sleeping are archaeologically detected activities which address the common goal of material survival. The abundant evidence for ritual within the patio group testifies to a concern on this level with social survival as well.

Material signs of the differentiation of patio groups, one from another, which would support their identification as independent identity units, are more elusive. The duplication of features in these units suggests comparable organization of independent households. However, the initial expectation that decorated ceramics would vary between patio groups, expressing their distinctive identities, was not supported. Samples of decorated Fine Buff ceramics from throughout the Terminal Classic site zone are indistinguishable on the basis of motifs employed or structure of design. Similarly, a comparison of Ulua Polychrome ceramics from CR-44 with those from Travesía, CR-212, and other Ulua Valley sites does not support the existence of motifs or design structure in the Late Classic unique to certain sites (Joyce 1987a).

The best evidence of differences in self-identification between patio groups may come from the distinctive contents of caches. Although generally containing the same kinds of materials (lithics and ceramic artifacts), no two caches were identical. In Group 1, caches incorporated a ground stone mano, a male figurine, a female figurine, and a whistle. The contemporary cache in Group 3A consisted of a groundstone bar and ball. In Group 4, two ceramic animal effigies and a biface were found, while caches in Groups 5B and 6A consisted of three and one chipped stone bifaces. Slight idiosyncratic variations on a common ritual practice are identifiable at the patio-group level. The three caches at CR-44 cannot be compared to the Terminal Classic examples, but instead may be compared to contemporary practice at the site of Travesía. While the jade bead and *Spondylus* cache is replicated at the two sites, other cached materials vary (Stone 1941:62, 66–67, 73), again suggesting independence within a common ideological framework.

The status of the patio-group cluster is more difficult to assess. A clear spatial unit of the site, patio-group clusters were not investigated thoroughly enough to provide adequate evidence for comparison. The analogy with the modern Zinacantec *sna* and waterhole groups and the similar Chorti *valles* suggests the possibility that these groups could have had a common orientation toward agricultural resources of land and water, undetectable in the archaeological record. The most distinctive activity of the Zinacantec waterhole group is its group-level ritual. The data from Teotihuacan and Tenochtitlan also indicate that clusters of residences may have shared common ritual facilities. Evidence for ritual at this level is elusive for Cerro Palenque.

The third level of coordination suggested is the small center, represented by Late Classic CR-44 and Terminal Classic CR-170 and CR-171. Defined in the first instance as spatial units, small centers are distinct from all other spatial groups in the presence of small plazas. Some of the activities carried out in plaza groups can be inferred from excavated remains. At CR-44, trash near the plaza included a high proportion of decorated serving vessels and a notable number and diversity of fine stone, bone, and shell costume elements. Since this plaza was located on the 240-meter-high peak of Cerro Palenque, it is unlikely that this trash was deposited far from its use location. These remains would suggest that the area around the plaza was used for specialized feasting and ritual with elaborately costumed participants. The fact that the plaza group is the one element distinctive of small centers suggests that the residents of patio groups in these centers were joined in the construction of common facilities for public ritual. In this way, small centers may be comparable to the hamlets of contemporary Zinacantan and the barrios and wards of Teotihuacan and Tenochtitlan.

Finally, the small centers form part of larger polities. The Terminal Classic polity is composed of CR-170, CR-171, and CR-157. The unique feature identifying this settlement unit is the great plaza group, with its ballcourt, main plaza, and series of terraced plazas. The main plaza and ballcourt form a unit suggestive of a template for public architecture common among the Lowland Maya (an identification suggested in Ashmore 1989:283). In the Maya template, these features are public ritual areas, with the ballcourt placed in a position between these public ritual areas and elite residential compounds (Ashmore 1986; 1989). Ballcourts and the ballgame play a role in mediating between the mundane and the supernatural (Gillespie 1985), a role replicated in the Maya site template. Artifacts from architectural fill in the plaza and ballcourt area of Terminal Classic Cerro Palenque suggest that activities included ritual (censers) and possibly feasting (serving vessels and faunal remains).

Large centers like CR-157 are the probable location of the residences of the rulers of independent polities. Several unique patio groups were mapped on the perimeter of the great plaza. One was directly connected to the southern end of the ballcourt. These were single patio groups incorporating two or three structures with basal dimensions around 100 square meters. Each of these singular plazas also included a central platform, which otherwise occurred only in multi-patio clusters. The combination of an unusual number of large structures, in the size range for residences, lack of small ancillary structures, and presence of unique ritual facilities suggests the distinctive nature of the residents of these patio groups.

Although decorated serving vessels did not provide evidence for distinctive self-identification on the patio-group level, differences in decoration of red-painted and incised jars can be identified between large centers of the Late and Terminal Classic Ulua Valley (Joyce 1987a). These jars were present throughout Cerro Palenque, in houses and central platforms in residential groups, and in public plazas. With their constricted necks and pairs of handles, these vessels are most appropriate for transporting and serving liquids. They would have been appropriate for brewing *chicha*, today an indispensable part of rituals practiced by the Lenca (Chapman 1985; 1986).

The Terminal Classic examples from Cerro Palenque share a distinct horizontal multiple wavy line painted pattern on the neck, not recorded for any other site in the Ulua Valley. Late Classic red-painted and incised jars from Travesía, Santa Rita, and Las Flores also vary in design and form. The examples from Late Classic Cerro Palenque, CR-44, are identical in form and decoration to those from Travesía. As a small center, CR-44 should be part of a polity centered on a larger contemporary settlement. In addition to the decoration of painted jars, CR-44 and Travesía also share a unique sculptural tradition, producing anthropomorphic slabs with inverted Christmas tree outlines and goggle eyes (Stone 1941: Fig. 49). It appears that the decoration of possible brewing jars may express a common identity at the level of the polity, also reflected in the maintenance of distinctive sculptural traditions.

The sites assumed to be the centers of independent polities in the valley do yield evidence of cross-cutting identity groups. Most obvious is the identity expressed in the shared tradition of decoration of the Ulua Polychromes. Variation in these highly elaborated ceramics is seen on a regional level, on which examples from the Ulua Valley and Lake Yojoa can be distinguished (Viel 1978; Joyce n.d.). This level of variation in Ulua Polychrome decoration may mark higher-order operating units linking the large centers in the Ulua Valley and distinguishing them from those in the Lake Yojoa area. The often-remarked parallels in design structure between Ulua Polychromes and Lowland Maya polychromes, particularly those of Belize and the Peten, in the Late Classic (Gordon 1898b; Vaillant 1927; Strong, Kidder, and Paul 1938; Stone 1957; 1970; Robinson 1978; Viel 1978; Joyce 1985; 1986; 1987a; 1988a; 1988b; n.d.; Sheptak

1987a) may indicate the existence of a much higher order identity group.

The common interests of the identity units which expressed their unity in these media will be considered in more detail later. First, the data from Cerro Palenque must be reconsidered as a source of information about the kind of interactions that took place between the different identity units that formed the precolumbian community.

Social Relationships within Cerro Palenque

The individual patio-group-centered households at Cerro Palenque, each replicating the same kinds of activities, are independent, comparable units. Through coordination, they may have formed a single class within the community. However, the distribution of scarce materials between the Terminal Classic patio groups excavated suggests that residents of some households were more privileged materially, perhaps reflecting centralization and the emergence of distinct social strata within the site. Even within patio groups there are possible indications of greater and lesser access to exotic goods, suggesting that the household itself may have been hierarchically organized.

Lithics provide the evidence for these inferences. In order to measure differences in access to scarce goods, it is necessary to control for variation due to different activities and consequently different kinds and proportions of artifacts appropriate to distinct tasks. This requirement identifies the patio group as the lowest-level unit appropriate for comparison. Individual structures clearly were the locus of distinctive activities marked by different numbers of artifacts, variation not reflecting distinct status.

Chipped stone tools are a natural body of evidence for discussion of differential status, since in lithics, unlike ceramics, much of the variation is not apparently related to function. Obsidian and local cherts and quartzites used for blade and biface production are functionally indistinguishable. The proportion of obsidian to local materials reflects differential access to imported materials.

The proportions of exotic to local materials were tabulated for each group, based on total cutting edge of blades and total numbers of bifaces represented in whole or part (Table 5). Comparisons between the contemporary patio groups of Terminal Classic Cerro Palenque suggest that more central location with respect to the great plaza of CR-157 is associated with greater access to exotic stone. The small sample size from Group 4 led to its exclusion from this comparison; all of the blades recovered here were obsidian, while the single biface was chert. Centrally located Group 1 had the highest proportions of obsidian; over half of the blades and the biface recovered from this group were of exotic stone. The other four patio groups, all located more peripherally, had much lower proportions of obsidian: 20 to 30 percent of blades, and 40 to 50 percent of bifaces. These frequencies do not diverge significantly from those for Terminal Classic Cerro Palenque as a whole: 33.6 percent of blades and 44.4 percent of bifaces in the entire Terminal Classic site zone were composed of exotic stone.

The suggestion that the residents of Group 1 had greater access than others to exotic materials is supported by other data as well. Domestic grinding stones throughout the site were made of basalt lava, available within the Ulua Valley but not directly at Cerro Palenque. Almost 60 percent of the basalt-lava tools recovered in the Terminal Classic site zone were from Group 1 (Table 6). Group 1 also incorporated exotic stone in architecture: basalt lava for a step and chlorite schist as part of the central platform. These materials were otherwise used only in nonresidential construction: chlorite schist and basalt lava in the isolated northern structure of CR-157, and basalt lava in the ballcourt.

The household represented by Group 1 appears to have been economically privileged, and might have housed members of the community in a position of power over the other Terminal Classic residential groups tested. The fact that this group was the only one

Table 6. *Proportions of ground basalt-lava tools by group*

Group	Metates	Manos	Other	% of Total
CR-157	10	8	4	100
Group 1	4	6	3	59.1
Group 3A, B	3	0	1	18.2
Group 4	0	0	0	0
Group 5A, B	2	1	0	13.6
Group 6A, B	1	1	0	9.1
CR-44	3	1	0	100
Group 2	1	0	0	25
Test pits	2	1	0	75

In addition to these ground basalt-lava tools, six other ground stone artifacts were recovered. A small celt (Group 3B) and a barkbeater (Group 5A) were made of unidentified fine-grained materials. A limestone ball (Group 4) and a limestone bar and ball (Group 3B) were found in caches. A section from a rimmed limestone metate was found in Group 3.

sampled that was near the main plaza groups of the site and the use in this group alone of architectural materials otherwise limited to nonresidential architecture suggest that members of the household may have been more closely involved with the ritual activities carried out in the main plaza than residents of other groups.

No other Terminal Classic patio group showed such marked access to exotic lithics as Group 1. Only one Late Classic patio group was excavated, and it could not be compared with the Terminal Classic examples since the absolute proportion of obsidian in Late Classic contexts was much higher. However, in both Late Classic and Terminal Classic patio groups, differential proportions of local and exotic lithic materials were noted within individual patio groups. These differences may also reflect centralization, in this case among the inhabitants of the patio-centered group.

In most cases, variation in proportion of materials between structures within patio groups could be explained by the different kinds of activities represented at different locations. However, comparisons of structures which provided evidence for the entire range of domestic activities suggest that in two cases the individuals housed in structures with benches made greater use of more exotic lithic materials than individuals housed in structures lacking benches but of comparable size located in the same group. In Terminal Classic Group 1, 70 percent of the chipped stone (using cutting edge of blades as the measure) at the northern structure, with its built-in bench, was obsidian. The proportion of obsidian in the simpler structure on the east side of the patio was between 40 and 45 percent. The bench itself represents greater labor investment in the northern structure, which was also provided with a well-worked basalt-lava step. The eastern structure was constructed solely of cobbles.

Although the proportion of obsidian to non-obsidian chipped stone in Late Classic Group 2 is less variable, the presence of two categories of obsidian allows similar comparison between the northern and southern structures. The southern structure, with built-in bench, had 20 percent green obsidian, while the northern structure facing it, lacking a bench and with signs only of perishable walls, had only the more common black obsidian. The southern structure included not only the bench but also elaborate sculptured stone formerly incorporated in an upper façade.

The individual patio groups and clusters at Cerro Palenque appear to be the residences of social units carrying out the same range of activities, but having variable access to scarce resources. Within indi-

vidual patio groups, dwellings with built-in furniture may mark especially privileged individuals. Similar suggestions have been made for
the sites of La Ceiba (Benyo 1986) and Copan (Hendon 1987). At La
Ceiba, one structure within individual patio groups was consistently larger. This structure also proved to have been among the
earliest established, and often contained burials. Julie C. Benyo
(1986:251–253) labels these "founder" structures, suggesting they
represent the dwelling of the founder of the household. Ethnographic
analogy supports the greater elaboration of the house of the eldest,
founding member of extended family households, for example among
the Chorti (Wisdom 1940). At Copan, one structure in each group
was always more elaborately constructed than others. This "dominant" structure (Hendon 1987:535–539) was also the locus of sculpture (if it occurred), tombs, and distinctive artifacts. Like Benyo,
Julia Hendon suggests these structures may have been the residence
of the head of the extended family housed in the group.

Residence adjacent to the public civic-ceremonial zone of Terminal
Classic Cerro Palenque is associated with the most clearly marked
differential access to resources. The basis for this privilege, and by
implication for centralization within the community, may have been
participation in the activities represented by the great plaza and
ballcourt. Ethnohistoric reports of the Conquest Period Maya (Landa
1973:28) state that the dwellings of the elite were concentrated
close to the public architecture around the plaza. An analysis of the
distribution of ceramics at the Postclassic site of Naco (Wonderley
1981) found a concentric distribution around the main plaza with
progressively more exotic, rarer materials nearer the center. Although other studies (Chase 1986:362–367) have failed to detect
such concentric patterning, Cerro Palenque clearly would not be
unique in this regard.

Both of these patterns, the identification of the zone around the
great plaza as distinctive and the identification within patio groups
of a dominant structure, can be supported by analysis of settlement
data for unexcavated structures of Cerro Palenque. Without excavation, the only attributes available for analysis are those of gross
scale. The evaluation of the scale of patios, individual mounds, patio
groups, and clusters has been discussed in the previous chapter. Two
classes of structures with base area of ca. 50 and ca. 100 square meters were detected in this analysis. All excavated examples in this
size range were found to have evidence for the full range of activities
represented at the site. By analogy with contemporary ethnographic
examples, these large structures are identifiable as dwellings, associ-

ated with smaller special-purpose structures in extended family households.

The spatial distribution within the Terminal Classic site of the larger and smaller dwelling-size structures is not random. All examples of the larger dwellings are among those patio groups closest to the main plaza of CR-157. One such group is directly southeast of the ballcourt, linked to it by a raised terrace. Four of the large structures define a single patio, 15 meters on a side, centered by a low platform.

Even more than the excavated Group 1, these large-dwelling patio groups suggest residences of people who carry out activities linked to the specialized architecture of the main plaza. Patio groups with large dwellings near the great plaza are not part of clusters. Several examples have a low central platform, like the excavated platforms suggested as locations of patio-group rituals. With their larger dwellings, single-patio-group structure, and high proportion of central platforms, the larger-dwelling patio groups concentrated near the great plaza of CR-157 suggest a distinctive use of this area.

The existence of a "principal dwelling" in each patio group or cluster is also suggested by a consideration of the size distribution of structures within the Terminal Classic site zone. Each of the excavated examples was the tallest nonmonumental structure in its group. (Monumental structures, those 2.5 meters or taller in height, rarely occur in patio groups. The sole excavated example, in Group 2, was clearly used primarily for ritual.) The distribution of the height and base area of large structures was plotted by patio group. In each patio, the largest structure in terms of base dimensions is generally also the tallest. In each cluster, one patio group has the largest and tallest structures. In any cluster, only this patio had a low central platform. The ritual activities practiced at these low platforms (like those represented in the excavated examples) were under the control of a limited number of households, housed in the largest and most elaborate architectural features. The patio and cluster, by implication, were centralized units with respect to these rituals.

As in the contemporary case of Zinacantan (Vogt 1969:127–149), the internal organization of Cerro Palenque can be interpreted as a series of centralized units, organized hierarchically in ever more inclusive groups carrying out joint ritual activities. Each of the minimal units, the patio groups, provided evidence for the full range of activities noted at the site; thus these may be interpreted as households with equivalent functions. The differences between patio groups and clusters were not expressed in any form recognized in the material excavated. Instead, the entire site shared specific ceramic decoration which distinguished the site as a whole from others and linked the inhabitants of patio groups and clusters.

An assertion of common identity within the site, coupled with evidence of distinction in access to economic resources, invites further comparison to the Zinacantec case. In Zinacantan, no elite class is acknowledged, and each family in theory has equal possibility to gain status through civil-ritual service (Cancian 1965). Nonetheless, measures of the concentration of economic resources found that higher-status positions and greater economic resources were concentrated in a few families, which in turn were linked by close marriage ties (Cancian 1965: 116–117).

At Cerro Palenque the comparable patio units are in theory of equivalent rank: they have evidence for the same range of activities, the size and elaboration of structures is not markedly different, and similar ceramic decoration is typical of all patio groups. In practice, however, these groups show variation in access to scarce resources. Those patio groups in closest proximity to the center of ritual activities are distinctive, with larger structures, more specialized ritual facilities, and greater access to exotic materials, including those otherwise reserved for public architecture. Within the patio group (presumably representing an extended family household), distinctions in seniority may be represented by the variation between principal and secondary dwellings.

As members of a single community, the inhabitants of Cerro Palenque were involved in social relationships with the population of other contemporary sites. The nature of these relationships can be clarified by identifying evidence of asserted membership in an identity group and identifying the objects or goals around which these higher-order identity units were organized. The discussion of interaction within the site has explored the dynamic dimension of the units of social structure identified in the previous chapter. The discussion of interaction between Cerro Palenque and other sites will add a dynamic to the brief discussion of political structure which ended that chapter.

Coordination and Centralization in the Ulua Valley

Cerro Palenque in the Late Classic was a small center, like many others in the Ulua Valley. Its shared sculptural and ceramic styles suggest it may have been part of a centralized polity whose large center was Travesía. In the Terminal Classic period, in contrast, Cerro Palenque was itself an independent large center, incorporating at least two small centers within its contiguous boundaries. Details of ceramic decoration document a common identity within the site and its contrast with contemporary sites along the Ulua River.

The common goals of the centralized polities to which Late Classic and Terminal Classic Cerro Palenque belonged must have been complex. The clearest evidence available relates to the practice of ritual on this level. The large plaza and ballcourt complexes of Travesía and CR-157 were presumably stages for ritual action. Artifactual evidence from Cerro Palenque suggests that these rituals included blood-letting, communal feasting, and masked dancing. Redistribution of exotic goods may also have been centralized on this level, as suggested by the differential distribution of the imperishable lithic resources discussed previously. Other goods possibly subject to redistribution within the centers may have been perishable, including for example luxury foods such as cacao. The acquisition of exotic goods was also apparently centralized under the control of individual polities.

A final possible common orientation of the large-center-based polities may have been the control of agricultural land and agricultural production. Robinson (1983) suggests that the projected populations of east-valley-edge polities would have been close to the carrying capacity of the land. She has employed a model based on agricultural colonization to explain the observed pattern of development of settlement on the east valley edge. Pope (1985:158–171; 1987) argues that the location of settlements in the Ulua Valley during the Classic Period is not determined by local agricultural potential. He suggests (1985:168–170) that agricultural support for large settlements might have been derived through redistribution of the produce from more desirable land, implying the involvement of political authorities in subsistence. Similarly, ethnohistoric sources suggest that individual polities based in large centers were the unit which coordinated control of agricultural land among the sixteenth-century Lenca (Chapman 1978:23–27).

Adams (1975:210–211) notes that centralization of a unit "usually occurs as a part of the coordination of that unit with other units," when identity units in structurally similar positions recognize a common goal. The superordinate elite of Terminal Classic Cerro Palenque, and of the Travesía–Cerro Palenque polity of the

Late Classic, would form coordinate identity units with the structurally similar elites of other large centers. Evidence for this relationship does exist, and common orienting goals may be suggested.

Ceramic decoration, specifically represented in elaborate red-painted and incised jars appropriate for brewing and serving beverages, was noted as one medium for the expression of center-level identity. The sculptural tradition of Late Classic Travesía and Cerro Palenque also embodies an identity between these two communities. The coordinate identity group which linked the distinct centralized polities of the Ulua Valley may also be expressed in variation in material symbolism.

In the Late Classic Period, the Ulua Polychrome style of decorated serving vessels throughout the Ulua Valley manifests a high degree of homogeneity (Viel 1978:281; Joyce 1987a). The Travesía and Santana class Ulua Polychromes of Travesía, Curruste, Santana, and Las Flores carry identical motifs in identical design organization. The boundary of this shared network of Ulua Polychrome design divides the entire Ulua floodplain from the Lake Yojoa region to the south, a contrast embodied in the definition of Travesía and Yojoa classes of Ulua Polychromes (Viel 1978:203–230). The Naco Valley to the west has a distinct, non-Ulua Polychrome tradition at the same time (Urban 1986a; Urban and Schortman 1988), as does the Sulaco Valley south and east (Hirth 1988, Kennedy 1982a). In each of these cases, the polychrome style is regional, not limited to a single site. In each case, polychrome decoration is applied to serving vessels. Finally, in all of these areas, the polychrome-decorated pottery is a service ware distributed throughout all levels of the settlement hierarchy.

The Ulua Polychrome Travesía and Yojoa substyles, and other polychrome styles of neighboring regions in the Late Classic, may be viewed as a medium of communication of a shared symbol system, in turn representing a shared belief system linking the sites within a region in a coordinate network. As serving vessels, they suggest that the behavior through which this common regional identity was expressed was common meals, or feasting (cf. Wonderley 1986a; 1987; 1988). The distribution of polychrome-decorated serving vessels to all levels of the settlement hierarchy may itself represent one of the means by which the superordinate elites engaged the subordinate populace in the common goals of a centralized polity. Distribution of other goods might have accompanied the feasts during which local elites gave their dependents examples of these finely decorated vessels.

Ethnographic data suggest that Lenca rituals, organized on a community level, involved this kind of feasting, accompanied by the drinking of beverages such as *chicha* and cacao (Chapman 1978: 35–36; 1985). Reciprocal visits between communities, called *guancasco*, maintained regional coordination (Adams 1957:618–623; Chapman 1978:30; 1986:133–146; Stone 1948).

The symbols painted on the vessels reflect the ideological content which in fact formed the basis for the interaction of the coordinate group. Anthropological analyses of such symbolism have proceeded from two complementary positions. Information theory has been applied to argue that all expressive culture carries messages, whether explicit or implicit (Wobst 1977). The statement that the decorated ceramic vessels connote different identity units follows this line of reasoning. At the same time, structural analyses suggest that the *contrast* between different groups in a domain is, by itself, not only an indication of their distinctiveness but a means of reinforcing it (Lévi-Strauss 1976). An emphasis on variation within the ceramic decorative traditions follows from this line of reasoning.

To say that ceramic designs reflect ideology, however, is distinct from these positions. This statement assumes that the particular symbols employed in decoration have referents which (to members of the culture originating the symbol) relate in some way (metaphorically or metonymically) to the kind of beliefs rehearsed when the ceramic vessels were used (Turner 1975:151–159). It follows that the content of the motifs, not simply their deployment in contrasting fashion, is of some interest (cf. Hodder 1986:121–122). I suggest a possible, speculative interpretation of the content of the two traditions of ceramic decoration which appear to represent identity units in Late and Terminal Classic Period Cerro Palenque.

The red-painted and incised jars produced in Late Classic and Terminal Classic Cerro Palenque are decorated with geometric motifs. Most characteristic are designs composed of multiple elements repeated in a regular fashion. In the Late Classic, these include groups of parallel wavy incised lines and painted multi-line lattices. In the Terminal Classic, only sets of horizontal wavy painted lines are found. An emphasis on multi-line decoration in ceramics is ancient in the area, established in the Late Formative in Usulutan resist ceramics. The use and elaboration of multi-line designs by much later Ulua Valley peoples may invoke the autochthonous nature of such decoration. Indigenous multi-element linear decoration (regardless of medium or means of execution) may be associated with social units emphasizing solidarity as a localized unit (the community).

This is in vivid contrast to the designs of the Ulua Polychrome tradition. Although forms, slip, and paint all have their origin in the same Usulutan decorated serving vessel tradition of the Late Formative, Ulua Polychromes are distinguished by a suite of design elements which from their inception includes elaborately costumed human figures and repeated profile head glyph forms. In the Late Classic, the major motifs of Ulua Polychromes include an anthropomorphic monkey; a waterbird often shown with a fish in its beak; human figures in processions, on thrones, confronting birds perched on other objects, or emerging from serpents; and jaguars, all themes comparable to contemporary Lowland Maya polychromes (Joyce n.d.; Robinson 1978). At a minimum, the message of these polychrome designs would include foreignness, the esoteric, and quite probably associations with the highly centralized polities of the Lowland Maya. The water imagery might have been associated with depictions of the underworld, and human figures emerging from serpents might have been associated with ancestors or other supernatural beings, in both cases the content of these designs on Lowland Maya ceramics.

The red-painted jars emphasize autochthonous traditions of decoration; the Ulua Polychromes represent a claim to affiliation with the wider world encompassed by Late Classic polychromes of Lowland Maya affiliation. The red-painted jar tradition embodies local-level identity, while the Ulua Polychromes stand for the regional-level coordinate group composed of hierarchically organized polities.

In the Terminal Classic Ulua Valley, a similar dichotomy exists between the autochthonous, multi-line-decorated red jars and the decorated serving vessels which replaced the Ulua Polychromes: Tehuma Fine Buff ceramics. Examples of Tehuma Fine Buff ceramics from many sites along the rivers in the Terminal Classic Period (including Travesía, Las Flores, Santa Rita, and Cerro Palenque) are indistinguishable on the basis of motifs or design structure. The motifs themselves, glyphic and geometric bands, are related to the Altar Ceramic Group of the Usumacinta drainage in the western Maya Lowlands (Joyce 1987c).

Altar Group designs, typified by the type Pabellon Modelled-Carved, also depict human beings, typically in confrontation, a circumstance interpreted as evidence for their use by warlike peoples moving into the area (Sabloff 1973:125–131). This aspect of the iconography is not carried over into the analogous Tehuma Fine Buff ceramics of the Ulua Valley, perhaps because the makers of these vessels were not invaders, but established local elites. Although the precise source and nature of the symbolism has changed, the Terminal Classic Tehuma Fine Buff ceramics have the same generic relationship to Lowland Maya ceramic traditions as did the Ulua Polychromes. Like the Ulua Polychromes, Tehuma Fine Buff ceramics assert a difference between the local population and the elite, linking the latter group with Maya peoples.

The content of the major surviving media for asserting regional coordinate identity ultimately testifies to links with a much wider area of Mesoamerica. It suggests the kinds of concerns which must have united the participants in this valley-wide coordinate group. Reciprocal feasting, like that associated with the *guancasco,* may have provided an opportunity to resolve regional conflicts in the absence of a higher authority. It may also, like the *guancasco,* have served as a mutual acknowledgment of boundaries of control of land. However, the use of symbolism allied with the wider Maya world suggests that the coordinate identity group may also have facilitated the movement of goods from that world into the local system. Possession and use of these complex decorated ceramics was concrete evidence by the coordinated regional elites of their access to a world unavailable to the majority of the population, except through centralized structures headed by the elites.

Cerro Palenque and the Maya Lowlands

The regional coordinate group which maintained and used Ulua Polychromes in the Late Classic and Fine Buff ceramics in the Terminal Classic was itself part of a wider coordinate linkage system, a network of interaction linking Honduran and Lowland Maya sites. Through this network flowed information, resulting in shared beliefs and ritual practices, such as the ballgame, bloodletting, and caching of jade and *Spondylus.* Through this network also flowed the exotic goods, such as obsidian, which were redistributed through local centralized structures. The final concern of this chapter is the elucidation of the evidence for this coordinate network, its asserted basis of identity and common orientation.

The evidence for shared values and beliefs which link Honduran and Lowland Maya sites includes a number of kinds of materials. Most abundant are decorated ceramics, initially polychrome, later fine paste. Rarer, but equally significant, are the spread of shell, jade, obsidian, and other fine stone used in restricted, often ritual, contexts. Ulua Polychrome ceramics, as has been noted, have a series of motifs closely related to contemporary Lowland Maya polychromes. These motifs are most closely paralleled in northern Belize, especially at the site of Altun Ha (Joyce 1986; n.d.; Sheptak 1987a).

Tehuma Fine Buff ceramics of the Terminal Classic may similarly be assigned a close relationship with Altar Fine Orange of the Usumacinta drainage, especially the site of Seibal (Joyce 1987c; Sabloff 1975).

The ceramics do not appear to have been exchanged through the proposed coordinate network. Local development of analogous types resulted from the spread of shared values expressed in this medium. However, the coordinate network need not be considered simply a means of transmission of information: jade, shell, obsidian, and carved Ulua Marble vessels were distributed throughout this area, presumably by means of inter-elite exchange facilitated by this network (Joyce 1986). Jade found at Cerro Palenque (although not subjected to compositional analysis) is most likely from the Motagua Valley sources which were exploited by the Late Classic site of Guaytan (Walters 1980). Obsidian identified from Classic Period contexts in the Ulua Valley (including Terminal Classic Cerro Palenque) is from the Ixtepeque source on the El Salvador–Guatemala border, while Preclassic samples stemmed from the southern Honduran La Esperanza source which returned to prominence in the Early Postclassic (Pope 1985:138; 1987:110–112). Ixtepeque obsidian may have entered the north coastal network through the Motagua Valley (Hammond 1972; 1976). It has been suggested that exchange in both jade and Ixtepeque obsidian was controlled by Quirigua (Sharer 1980; Stross et al. 1983). Evidence that exchange of material goods through this coordinate network was not a one-way traffic is provided by the presence at Altun Ha, San José, and Uaxactun of carved Ulua Marble vases, dated to the Terminal Classic (Kidder 1947:36–37, Fig. 20; J. E. S. Thompson 1939:167, Fig. 92p; Pendergast 1967), and perhaps liquid mercury, found in a Terminal Classic ballcourt at Lamanai (Pendergast 1986:229–230). Other material goods found throughout this area which may have moved from the frontier to the Maya heartland include *Spondylus* (thorny oyster) from Pacific waters (Andrews IV 1969; Feldman 1974).

Green obsidian, presumed to originate in Central Mexico, may have entered the Classic Period network from Lowland sites of the Peten or Belize, such as Tikal, Becan, or Altun Ha (Moholy-Nagy 1976; Rovner 1976; Pendergast 1971). The same sources may account for the presence in Late Classic Cerro Palenque of a black, eared obsidian biface recognized as a Lowland Maya version of a Central Mexican pattern (Tolstoy 1971:Fig. 2–3; Moholy-Nagy 1976), at the same time that some architectural façades at Cerro Palenque were built in a version of the talud-tablero profile which originated in Mexico.

More important than the source of these patterns, however, are their implications for the adoption of common ideological orientations and resulting behavior. The coordinate network was more than an exchange system which ensured the provision of elite sumptuary goods, however crucial that role may have been (Freidel 1979). It was also the means by which a common cosmology and ritual were spread among the elites of Lowland Maya and Honduran polities of the Late Classic. Common religion provided a basis for these elites to recognize each other as part of a single identity group.

The ballgame and the pattern of caching jade beads and *Spondylus* shell are two examples of rituals spread through the coordinate network which linked Honduran and Lowland Maya polities. The ritual ballgame is represented by distinctive ballcourts. Classic Period examples from Honduras were found in the Ulua and Naco valleys, at Lake Yojoa, west in the middle Ulua Valley, and in the Comayagua Valley. Travesía in the Late Classic and Cerro Palenque in the Terminal Classic each have ballcourts.

The Cerro Palenque Terminal Classic ballcourt and its closely related coeval from Los Naranjos may represent a development from the Late Classic Copan model toward a model represented in greatest number in Highland Guatemala during the Late Classic and Early Postclassic. The Late Classic Copan model seems to have been followed by the builders of the ballcourt at La Sierra in the Naco Valley (Henderson et al. 1979) and of the ballcourt at Travesía (Stone 1941). The shift from the Copan pattern is accomplished by adding a low bench to the range, a shift also noted at the contemporary sites of San José, Belize, and Coba (Quirarte 1977).

The ballgame reflected a complex set of cosmological beliefs interpreted on the basis of associated sculptural art in Mesoamerica (Gillespie 1985; M. E. Miller and Houston 1987; Schele and Miller 1986:241−264). Honduran ballcourts, with the exception of that at Copan, do not offer such evidence, and so the details of local views of this ritual game are uncertain. However, for the Maya, who must have been the source of this ritual for Hondurans, one particularly pertinent theme is the importance of ballgame playing as part of the role of the ancestral Hero Twins in the *Popol Vuh* (Tedlock 1985), who provided the archetype for Late Classic Maya elites. The importance of ballcourts in Postclassic Maya sites of highland Guatemala presumably reflects this fact. The parallels of the Cerro Palenque ballcourt with those of contemporary Highland Guatemala suggest that a similar belief and function may have been relevant to the elite of Cerro Palenque. It is particularly striking that both areas have examples of ballcourts with single markers, rather than paired markers; and that ballcourts in both areas connect to a plaza group with a central altar platform, presumably a stage for part of the ballgame ritual. Such close correspondences in the form of the stage suggest that the rituals enacted may have been quite similar.

The caching of jade beads in *Spondylus* shells, often augmented by cinnabar red pigment, is a second type of ritual behavior whose distribution crosses the boundary between Lowland Maya and Honduran archaeological regions. The obvious juxtaposition of red and green in these caches, along with the marine origin of the shell, suggests that the symbolism of this cache relates to the ocean/underworld equivalence identified in Maya belief (Rands 1955; A. G. Miller 1982). Early Classic ocean water is depicted as a red liquid, perhaps equivalent to blood. The spines of the thorny oyster may recall autosacrifice as a means of establishing contact with the supernatural world, whose marine aspect is the source of primordial bloodletting instruments, shark's teeth and stingray spines. The replication of this cache pattern need not imply that the background of belief elaborated in Maya thought was accepted by the Honduran elites. Nevertheless, like the ballgame, Maya beliefs surrounding the watery underworld and bloodletting are intimately connected with validation of elite status.

Mechanisms of the coordinate network can only be suggested. Clear evidence of exchange of exotic goods has been noted. The ballgame and shared cache patterns may indicate a common elite religion, relating both Maya and Honduran elites as members of a class with supernatural ancestry distinct from subordinate commoners. Intermarriage, known to have linked distinct Maya polities (e.g., J. Marcus 1976; Mathews 1980), may have extended throughout the network as well. Maya intermarriage is known from the direct evidence of inscriptions, evidence not available for Honduran archaeological sites. However, elite burials may provide indications of foreign origin of elite individuals. Burials from Copan which included Ulua Polychromes, and others incorporating Altun Ha polychromes, may suggest widespread kinship links (Joyce 1985:449–455; cf. Longyear 1952; Coggins 1988).

The common goal of the coordinate network which linked Honduran and Lowland Maya elites appears to have been political. No evidence exists that large-scale movement of basic subsistence goods was part of this network. Although obsidian may have moved through this network, obsidian is not a necessity (particularly at Cerro Palenque with its abundant cherts and quartzites), and centralized control would not be necessary for the acquisition of obsidian from local sources (see Sorenson 1985). The coordinate network did facilitate the movement of exotic goods used by the elite, such as jade and Pacific shell, and obsidian which moved through this system was apparently subject to hierarchically controlled redistribution. Both the consumption of exotic goods by the elite and the redistribution of exotic goods to the population at large would reinforce the status of the elite. The definition of the elite as separate from the subordinate population may have been the principal goal of the identity group represented by the coordinate network, and the common orientation may have been the shared need to continually reinforce elite status.

Mary W. Helms (1979; 1988:131–171) has suggested that the acquisition of esoteric knowledge was a major means for precolumbian elites to mark themselves as different and more powerful than the population at large. This can be seen as a particular case of the model of social power (Adams 1975) outlined at the beginning of this chapter. Provided that the elite and commoners both recognize such connections (and the knowledge they represent) as worthwhile, the fact that elites had access to the greater Mesoamerican world could have placed them in a position of power over the subordinate population. Evidenced in concrete form in material goods which came from outside the local sphere and reinforced in ritual practices whose definition originated elsewhere, influencing the common population through the occasional distribution of those rare goods and the enactment of those rituals, the membership of the Honduran elite in a coordinate identity group would have been a major source of reinforcement of their privileged position.

Cerro Palenque was clearly a complex community. Individual households, recognizing common ground, formed the basis for the community. At the same time, a small elite used a variety of means to reinforce their difference from the majority of the population and their commonality with the elites of other communities throughout Honduras and southern Mesoamerica. The balance between coordination and centralization was by no means stable. The dynamic development of Cerro Palenque through time, touched on in previous chapters, is a direct consequence of this instability, and the subject of the next chapter.

Chapter 6. Social Dynamics: Transformation

IN PREVIOUS chapters, the data from Cerro Palenque were reviewed and their structural patterns and implications for interaction were explored. The initial Late Classic site was a small center, perhaps part of a polity headed by Travesía. The material culture of this small center was lavish, incorporating unique sculpture and exotic goods from as far away as Central Mexico. In the Terminal Classic, this small center grew into the single largest community of the precolumbian Ulua Valley, with an extensive public ceremonial center. At the same time, the range of exotic goods, and their absolute proportions, shrank drastically. This shift in settlement and impoverishment in material goods took place as the indigenous polychrome style (affiliated with Lowland Maya polychrome styles such as that of Altun Ha) was replaced by temperless, incised ceramics inspired by contemporary western Maya traditions.

Organizationally, Cerro Palenque was composed of economically self-sufficient households, grouped into more inclusive clusters. The clusters, associated with large-scale architecture on plazas, made up small centers perhaps representing single hamlets, together comprising the community of Cerro Palenque. At each level of organization, the common identification of the residents was expressed in ritual. Material symbolic expression of distinctions in identity (primarily in the medium of decorated ceramics deployed in ritual feasting) was found on two levels, that of the community (contrasting with each other community) and that of the region as a whole. The regional identity united not the entire population, but the elites of different sites. This elite coordinate network extended beyond the bounds of the region to incorporate the elites of Lowland Maya sites, reinforcing the distinction between elite and commoners and the power of the former over the latter.

A full interpretation of the archaeology of Cerro Palenque must account for changes through time. The observed transformation must be understood in terms of the suggested units of organization and processes of interaction. This topic occupies the remainder of this chapter, adding the final historical dimension to the account of the life and development of Cerro Palenque.

Patterns of Change through Time at Cerro Palenque

Any attempt to interpret the transformation of the small Late Classic hilltop center to the extensive Terminal Classic center must account for a number of characteristics. First, the growth of the site was not accompanied by a change in the nature of the constituent units of the site. Second, the Terminal Classic site incorporated smaller centers within a single contiguous community. And third, the development of the larger Terminal Classic center was accompanied by an overall impoverishment of the material culture of the site.

The individual patio groups of Terminal Classic Cerro Palenque are identical in general size, features, and internal differentiation to Late Classic patio-groups from the Ulua Valley (Joyce and Sheptak 1983). The patio groups in the Terminal Classic continue to be organized in clusters. The only discernable difference between Terminal Classic Cerro Palenque and Late Classic sites might be the lesser density of patio groups and clusters. For example, patio groups of Copan and La Ceiba are composed of many more structures, sometimes assuming the appearance of a closed group. This difference, however, seems to reflect the truncation of the developmental cycle at Cerro Palenque, a Terminal Classic site which was abandoned fairly rapidly.

The most dramatic contrast between Terminal Classic Cerro Palenque and Late Classic sites of the Ulua Valley is the much greater number of the constituent patio-group units. Given the evidence for a relatively short period of occupation, the greater number of patio groups, and hence of residents, in the Terminal Classic site most probably reflects population nucleation, not population growth. Two lines of evidence suggest that this is in fact the case. First, although a number of centers along the Ulua River have evidence of occupation in the beginning of the Terminal Classic period, no other center continues to be occupied throughout the full Terminal Classic. Cerro Palenque appears to have been the sole center for population nucleation in the Terminal Classic, and may have attracted people from faltering centers such as Travesía. Second, the Terminal Classic community itself incorporates two small centers within the contiguous site zone, a degree of concentration of functions not noted in the Ulua Valley prior to this period.

The integration of the two small centers within the Terminal Classic site has been suggested both on the basis of the continuity of occupation between the small centers and the core of CR-157 and on the basis of the presence of complementary facilities. The small centers have small plazas ringed by three monumental structures. The main plaza of CR-157, in contrast, is twice as large as was typical of Late Classic sites, and included both long, low structures and more typical pyramidal monumental architecture. Most distinctive, only this plaza had a ballcourt.

The integration of the small centers in the Terminal Classic community is also suggested by the general relationship in the Late Classic Ulua Valley between the scale of the public architecture and plaza and the number of associated residential groups. The main plaza of CR-157 is twice as large as that of Late Classic centers, and with the inclusion of the small structures adjacent to the two smaller plazas, the number of residential groups is also double that of Late Classic centers. Without these, the construction of the plaza of CR-157 must be attributed to the same size population as Late Classic centers, suggesting a greater labor demand on the supporting population. Such a demand seems out of keeping with other evidence from Cerro Palenque, which depicts an elite impoverished with respect to their Late Classic predecessors.

The impoverishment of Terminal Classic Cerro Palenque is evident in both the lesser elaboration of architecture, and the decline in imperishable imported goods. No jade, no exotic shell, and proportionally little obsidian are found in the Terminal Classic excavations. Cut stone architecture is limited to a single basal course on part of the ballcourt and rare cut stone steps associated with otherwise cobble-constructed buildings. The impoverishment is most dramatically illustrated in the contrast between caches from Terminal Classic and Late Classic residential groups. In the Late Classic, Pacific *Spondylus* shell, jade, and obsidian formed these caches. In the Terminal Classic, most caches contained locally made ceramic artifacts, ground stone, or chert lithics.

The Processes of Change at Cerro Palenque

Terminal Classic Cerro Palenque represents the end of a trajectory of centralization in the Ulua Valley. As Adams (1975 : 77) discusses, centralization takes place in the context of confrontation between social groups which are not in a clear relationship of differential power. In the Classic Period, the largest centers in the Ulua Valley were potential competitors, apparently maintaining their individual autonomy. The elites of these communities entered into long-distance coordinate networks as one means to maintain their independent status.

While it is possible to discuss the long-distance contacts between Honduran and Lowland Maya sites as if these formed a single network, a more accurate description would emphasize the appearance of a series of overlapping networks forming a lattice. Each site is the center of a series of unique external links, and the lattice is built up of these overlapping networks. Long-distance contacts were established between individual pairs of sites or, more properly, between the elites of these pairs of sites.

The Late Classic Period pattern seems to have been to diversify external contacts. One obvious change in the Terminal Classic is the stronger focus on a single external link, that between Cerro Palenque and the Usumacinta drainage, represented by Seibal. Although initially a number of sites along the Ulua River have ceramic evidence of this long-distance contact, it soon narrows to a single focus. Terminal Classic Cerro Palenque emerges as the sole centralized polity of the Ulua Valley. Its population rises, apparently through nucleation of previously dispersed settlement. Cerro Palenque succeeds in the competition between centralized communities in the Ulua Valley. Nonetheless, this success does not seem to accompany the emergence of a new basis for centralization; rather, it reflects a change in the political organization of the external partners in coordinate networks.

Terminal Classic Cerro Palenque is a "primate center," a site an order of magnitude larger than any of its regional contemporaries (Johnson 1977). Primate center development has been associated with a particular kind of economy in studies of modern regional economic systems (C. A. Smith 1976), an economic model which makes sense when applied to Cerro Palenque.

In ethnographically described cases, primate center development is associated with the development of dendritic economies (C. A. Smith 1976 : 315–320; Schwimmer 1976; Appleby 1976; Bonsack

Kelley 1976). In dendritic economies, a series of centers are linked in a single network through which flow all exchanged goods. Each region in the dendritic economy has a single center, through which all exchange is centralized and in which the local elite is concentrated. Contemporary dendritic economies have been associated with the exploitation of a less developed region by a more developed polity for the monocrop production of a single resource. A foreign elite may be located in the center, or the local elite may identify with those of the more developed region, adopting material culture patterned on that region. While material flows out of the exploited region through the dendritic network, less flows back, and what does return is concentrated in the center itself. In formal economic terms, the presence of only a single market creates a monopoly in which the producers have no choice but to accept the disadvantageous terms offered by the elites controlling the export market.

Obviously, in a preindustrial society, such a model cannot be applied in full. However, it does have features which recommend the evaluation of its fit to Terminal Classic Cerro Palenque. Settlement primacy, a unique network focused on a single site, the presence in that site of an elite using material incorporating foreign symbolism, and the general impoverishment of the area are all features found in modern dendritic economies and present at Terminal Classic Cerro Palenque. In modern dendritic economies, these features have been associated with a particular economic system. In preindustrial societies, it is likely that economy and polity were inextricably linked and that the functions now analyzed as a separate economy were part of the workings of the sociopolitical system (Polanyi 1958; Firth 1963:122–154).

The diversified networks of the Late Classic (which were the means of transmission of goods over long distances) produced the same effect as multiple competitive market centers do in modern regional economic systems. Individual groups resident in smaller sites could become affiliated with one of a number of centers, and the centers consequently existed in a dynamic balance competing for the support of commoners. On a higher level, each center was able to draw on a number of external links for both material and ideological support.

In contrast, in the Terminal Classic, Cerro Palenque was the only viable center in the Ulua Valley, and residents of smaller sites were forced to live with their relationship to that center, or choose not to have access to the services represented by centers. In turn, the elite of Cerro Palenque, while no longer involved in competition with other centers, were also limited to a single external link which provided fewer exotic goods than was previously the case. Although the mechanism proposed was primarily political, the effects were similar to those seen in contemporary dendritic economic systems, where the mechanism is the market system.

Events outside the Ulua Valley must have been responsible for this change, which was exploited politically by Cerro Palenque, and which led to the material impoverishment of that site. The external links of the Late Classic Ulua Valley seem largely directed toward the Maya Lowlands through Belize. In the Terminal Classic, the Maya Lowlands were undergoing reorganization described succinctly as "an upward collapse" (Erasmus 1968, cited in Willey 1986 : 196). In the western lowlands, the drainage of the Usumacinta witnessed the probable invasion of a new group of people who appear to have tried to stabilize networks focused on sites such as Seibal and Altar de Sacrificios (Sabloff and Willey 1967; Willey 1973; J. E. S. Thompson 1970). These new elites have been identified as Mexicanized Maya of the Gulf Coast, who were involved in the exchange of economic resources between lowlands and highlands. Whether or not this model holds up, it is clear that centralized polities at Seibal and Altar de Sacrificios remained stable while other sites in the Maya Lowlands were experiencing an intensive disruption of political organization. Quite simply, most of the potential external partners in networks with the Ulua Valley failed at the end of the Classic Period.

The collapse of many Lowland Maya polities may account for the narrowing of the range of external partners available for links with Ulua Valley sites in the Terminal Classic. The reciprocal narrowing of connections to the Ulua Valley to a single link with Cerro Palenque may be due to two complementary factors: a change in the interests of the external Maya partner and the consequent increase in the importance of locally available resources.

Seibal in the Terminal Classic, it has been argued, was important to its new elite as an integral node on the supply route for goods which entered into a market system on the Gulf Coast (Sabloff and Willey 1967; J. E. S. Thompson 1970). If this is true, then the motives of the elite at Seibal were not primarily the establishment of a network of external contacts to support their elite status, but rather the stabilization of the supply of exchange goods. This shift provides a potential explanation for the concentration on a single site in each supply area, the feature diagnostic of the dendritic economy.

Other factors may be responsible for the emergence of Cerro Palenque as the particular site with external links in the Terminal Classic Ulua Valley. The amount of exotic materials entering the region was reduced. Sites along the river course were in general at a disadvantage, lacking lithic resources to replace the nonlocal obsidian which declined in supply. Cerro Palenque, on the other hand, was located in a hill zone with abundant chert and quartzite cobbles, which were used to replace the bulk of the obsidian formerly used for tools.

If Terminal Classic Cerro Palenque was, in fact, part of a dendritic economy ultimately linked to Seibal, what economic good might it have supplied for the market interests which presumably dominated this development? The most obvious candidate is cacao. This luxury good was produced in the Ulua Valley at the time of the Spanish Conquest (Bergmann 1969; Millon 1955). Ethnohistoric sources which describe the quality of cacao place the produce of the Ulua Valley in the most desirable category. Today, in Lenca ritual, grinding and drinking cacao is an act which expresses connection with the four quarters and the hierarchy between petitioners and practitioners (Chapman 1985). While the use of this perishable good cannot be definitively confirmed for the Late Classic, modeled ceramic cacao pods and figurines with cacao pod representations (Stone 1972 : 192) from the Valley do suggest its use. Cacao is the kind of good which could easily have circulated in a politically motivated network, since it had strong ritual importance. It could have passed into a market system as a medium of exchange, as was the case in the Postclassic among the Aztec.

If the model outlined here is valid, then the Terminal Classic emergence of Cerro Palenque depended on a reinterpretation of the purpose of the network linking Honduran and Lowland Maya sites by only one of the parties involved. While the elite of Cerro Palenque continued to use the coordinate linkage as a way to identify themselves as distinct from commoners, and as imbued with supernatural authority, the western Maya partners saw the same network as a means to acquire a market commodity. This difference in perception created the seed of the ultimate collapse of Cerro Palenque. The western Maya episode did not long continue, and when the elite of this area withdrew from the network, the elite of Cerro Palenque were left without an external link validating their separate status.

Chapter 7. An Interpretive Archaeography

IN THE preceding chapters, I have presented a particular interpretation of patterned material remains recovered through archaeological research at Cerro Palenque. I have tried to describe the evidence available from a number of different perspectives suggested by my research interests, resulting in a kind of "thick description" of the material remains of Cerro Palenque (Geertz 1973). My original research questions influenced both the kinds of information I sought, and the kinds of interpretations I have stressed. These interpretations revolve around three general concerns: how were the people of Cerro Palenque organized in groups? How did these groups interact with similar and different groups? And how did these groups of people and their interactions change through time?

More specifically, I have considered possible answers to these questions: What were the social and political institutions of Cerro Palenque? What were the changes between the Late Classic and the Terminal Classic, which accompanied the growth and nucleation of the site and changes in material culture? What processes resulted in these changes? How was Cerro Palenque linked to other areas around it?

The Constructed Interpretation: A Selective Overview

Different kinds of material remains have been used in order to address these questions. Settlement patterns within the site and within the region were examined as a source of information about variation in a series of residential, and perhaps social, units. Regularities in size ranges of individual structures, and size and composition of groups of structures, were assumed to be meaningful, indicating regularities in the use of space by hierarchically nested social groups. At least three distinct levels of settlement units within the site were identified. Individual structures were joined together in patio-centered groups. Patio-centered groups in turn formed part of larger clusters. These clusters of patio groups, along with distinctive architectural groups larger in scale but simpler in composition, formed a third level of differentiated settlement within the site.

These three levels of settlement clusters can be interpreted as distinctive residential units. Comparison with settlement patterns of ethnographically documented Zinacantan, ethnohistorically documented Tenochtitlan, and archaeologically documented Teotihuacan, indicates the possibility that the patio group represents the space occupied by a household, the cluster of patio groups forms a nucleated neighborhood, and these neighborhoods, together with public architectural zones, form small hamlets. No necessary correlation is suggested with any particular kind of kinship units. Although kinship is one means of defining bonds between members of the household, the most regular feature defining different settlement units is the recognition of commonality through the enactment of ritual.

Facilities for unifying ritual were identified at each level of settlement, with excavated examples extrapolated to structures with similar size and position within groups. Within some patio groups, a low central platform was located. Excavated examples yielded cached material, including lithics, jade, and shell (in Late Classic examples), and ceramic artifacts and lithics (in Terminal Classic examples). Other artifacts from these locations included chipped stone blades, fragments of ceramic censers, grinding stones, and fragments of large, elaborately decorated jars morphologically suited to serving and brewing beverages.

Although there was great variation in the individual contents of caches, they included chipped stone blades and bifaces and ideologically significant artifacts: the combination of jade bead and *Spondylus* shell, for example, associated with marine-underworld identifications, and the structurally complex set of figurines associating femaleness and ordinary tasks with the west and maleness and costumed ritual with the east. Together, these cached materials and the refuse from these locations suggest activities including burning of incense, bloodletting, drinking, and perhaps costumed dance.

The kinds of activities represented by central platforms form a single complex, but the precise details vary from group to group. Differentiation between the groups and singular identity of each group may be implied. While only a minority of patio groups mapped appear to have such central platforms, every excavated group produced at least one structure with an internal stone bench. Patterns of caching and refuse at these structures in part parallels that noted for the unique central platforms, and in groups lacking central platforms, ritual may have taken place within the house.

Caches were buried in benches or below the threshold. Like caches in central platforms, those in rooms with benches consisted of lithics, especially bifaces, and ceramic artifacts. The imagery of ceramic artifacts in these locations again hints at their meaning, like the pairing of effigies of jaguar and bird in Group 4.

Like the caches in central platforms, those in benches were varied. Structures with benches also yielded grinding stones, elaborately decorated jars, and blades, the artifacts common in central platforms, suggesting that the same activities may have been carried out in both kinds of locations. Censers, a clearly specialized ritual form, were found near one bench as well.

These two kinds of structures may have served as the focus for rituals on the level of the residential group which defined the group as an integrated whole distinct from other such groups. In contrast, few structures which could have formed a focus for ritual and differentiated identity of clusters of patio groups were excavated. Many examples of unusually tall structures were noted in mapping. A Late Classic example, integrated in a patio group, and a Terminal Classic example, located between clusters, were excavated. Each produced little in the way of domestic refuse, and much that was distinctive. The Late Classic example was ornamented with sculpture, and had large open rooms. The Terminal Classic example also was associated with sculpture, and had a unique facing material. Fragments from ornate ceramic censers were found in both cases, although the precise ornamentation differed. Like the central platforms excavated, these tall structures seem likely to have been sites of ritual. Similar anomalously tall structures are not found in every patio group, and may mark distinct clusters forming an intermediate, neighborhood-level social unit.

Most distinctive in the settlement pattern of Terminal Classic Cerro Palenque are three subdivisions, each consisting of clusters of patio groups adjacent to a large plaza ringed on three sides by long, tall structures. Both the size of the plaza and the size of the structures suggest they are distinct in function from the smaller patio groups. Based on comparisons with other known sites, these plaza groups can be regarded as probable public and ritual areas. They define a tripartite division of the continuous settlement of Terminal Classic Cerro Palenque.

The two subsidiary plazas are smaller and simpler than the single, major plaza which is central to the entire Terminal Classic site zone. While the smaller plazas open east, along the path of the sun, the great plaza opens south, the direction associated with the underworld, source of supernatural power. The central structure in the great plaza acts as an axis not only for the plaza, but for the entire site. Raised stone walkways lead north, the direction associated with the upperworld, and rise with the natural slope through a series of triadic plazas which echo the southern orientation of the great plaza. At the very end of the northern axis, a unique structure, facing south toward the natural hill, forms a complement to the southern location of the ballcourt, a passage from the great plaza to Cerro Palenque hill. These features conform to a recognized site plan which in the Maya area has been interpreted as a representation of cosmic and cardinal order. A number of arguments were presented to support the interpretation of the great plaza as a facility built for and used by the population of the entire site. Artifacts from excavations in the great plaza included censers and many ceramic serving vessels and jars, including unusual examples. Along with the known use of the ballcourt for the ritual ballgame, these remains suggest that the great plaza was also a site for the kinds of ritual behavior noted at all other levels of the settlement.

Regarding the patio groups as minimal residential units, and consequently as minimal economic units, excavated remains were used to propose that each household was probably independent, producing chipped stone tools for use within the group (indicated in many distinct locations within the group by the presence of cores, blades, and flakes of all sizes), and processing maize within the group (indicated by the presence of grinding tools). Patio groups produced evidence for specialized function structures, such as ritual platforms and probable storage rooms. In each group, structures with the largest area produced evidence for a wide range of tasks including food consumption. Some had built-in stone benches. These structures are interpreted as the main dwellings of the residential group. The number of dwellings per patio group is not high in the majority of cases, perhaps because the site had a truncated period of occupation and of development of multigeneration households.

Most of the excavated and mapped data reflected the presence of nested, increasingly inclusive settlement units, and could also be used to explore the political organization of the site. Excavated distributions of exotic and local lithic resources were asymmetric, presumably reflecting differential access to resources. The greatest proportion of exotic stone was noted in the patio group closest to the great plaza, perhaps suggesting a concentric model of settlement.

Higher-order settlement patterns, comparing the site to other spatially distinct sites in the Ulua Valley, allowed the recognition of at least three distinct levels of settlement. The simplest consisted only of patio groups or clusters of such groups. In some cases, clusters of patio groups were located adjacent to simple plaza groups with three flanking structures. Finally, a small minority of sites, with the largest number of associated patio groups, also include a large plaza ringed by differentiated structures, sometimes including a ballcourt. This three-level settlement hierarchy may reflect a series of centralized polities, with subordinate centers nested within the territory and under the control of the larger centers. In this scheme, Terminal Classic Cerro Palenque is at the top of a hierarchy, while Late Classic Cerro Palenque is a subordinate center. While there are many centers in the Late Classic settlement pattern (with the site of Travesía perhaps most closely related to Cerro Palenque in architecture, sculpture, and ceramics), Terminal Classic Cerro Palenque is unique. It is also much larger than its Late Classic counterparts, both in number of structures and in size of plaza and monumental architecture. While the Late Classic settlement pattern may reflect a number of competing polities of equal size and perhaps power, the Terminal Classic pattern testifies to the presence of a single centralized polity.

The growth of Cerro Palenque from Late to Terminal Classic is accompanied by a series of puzzling changes. The presence of all foreign goods declines. The chipped stone blade tool industry is adapted to abundant local cherts, quartzites, and chalcedonies. Cut stone is largely abandoned, even in such significant construction as the ballcourt. The elaborate and varied polychrome-painted serving vessels of the Late Classic are abandoned (although their use continues elsewhere in Honduras), and well-burnished, temperless, thin ceramics, decorated with incised and stamped decoration, take their place. While censer vessels continue to be decorated with appliqué, the scalloped and impressed geometric bands of Late Classic examples are replaced by spiked and human-effigy forms.

A simple model was constructed to account for these patterns. The maintenance of hierarchical distinctions between elite and non-elite in the Late Classic Ulua Valley would have required two inter-related processes. First, elites would have had to define themselves as a distinct group; and second, they would have had to identify themselves as in control of some objective of general interest to the population on which they depended. Both steps were accomplished by the elite adoption of Lowland Maya styles in material culture, symbolism, and presumably ideology. Manifest in the decoration of the elaborate serving vessels used by all members of the population for meals, including ritual feasts, contact with the Maya Lowlands by the elite was simultaneously a source for prized material goods (such as obsidian, jade, and shell), and a means to differentiate the elite from commoners.

The Terminal Classic material culture of Cerro Palenque similarly reflects the adaptation of material symbolism of the Maya Lowlands, specifically a western Maya tradition. Terminal Classic centralization, however, was focused on a single site, which in turn appears to have had a single external contact of overriding significance. The associated poverty of material culture may be indicative of a process associated with dendritic patterns in regional economic theory. As economic affairs were presumably simultaneously social and political affairs, the narrowing of external contacts to a single relationship in the Terminal Classic would have had not only economic but also political and social significance. While one source of support for elite position in the Ulua Valley, identification with foreign power, continued, the influx of material goods previously used in ritual and for redistribution was drastically reduced. This reduction in turn may reflect a distinct reinterpretation of the nature of the relationship on the part of the Lowland Maya partners, from a more generalized social and political connection to a more narrowly focused economic one.

Many of the suggestions offered in the course of this argument have revolved around the interpretation of the meaning of material symbolism. The motifs of Ulua Polychromes represent a subset of those found on Lowland Maya polychromes, especially those associated with the underworld, elite ancestry, and the importance of writing. The use of multi-line geometric motifs in ceramic decoration for over 1,000 years in the Ulua Valley may have served to indicate indigenous, autochthonous connections. The layout of the great plaza of Terminal Classic Cerro Palenque, and particularly of its ballcourt, suggests the form, if not the content, of Maya patterns of settlement in which north is associated with ancestors and supernatural beings, south with the secular world or underworld, and mediation between the two is achieved through the ballgame and its setting. Caching of stone tools and ceramic artifacts may demarcate cultural groupings. The depiction of male figures in feathered costume, birds, and jaguars may reflect a set of beliefs dimly reflected in modern Lenca traditions about a woman named "Flying Jaguar," who established the Lenca world and divided it among her three sons, and with the aid of lightning, turned into a bird and flew into the sky.

Interpretation and the Status of Archaeography

The interpretation offered here is based on the selection of certain characteristics relevant to a particular set of interests. The imputation of significance rests on the nature of patterned differences and similarities in these characteristics. In the end, this is only one of many possible interpretations of the archaeological remains from Cerro Palenque.

Archaeographies, or archaeological ethnographies, have the same status, as interpretations, as other ethnographies. They are dependent on observations of material patterning, rather than behavior, but their ultimate concern is the same: the coherent, intelligible explication of the articulation of culture, conceived of as a web of meanings specific to a particular place and time. The process is inferential; it "begins with a set of (presumptive) signifiers and attempts to place them within an intelligible frame" (Geertz 1973 : 26).

Unlike the ethnography accomplished by the contemporary observation of behavior, the archaeological ethnography is based on observation of patterns of material remains. These patterns, established by the behavior of the vanished members of past societies, were meaningfully constituted and provide the grounding of archaeological interpretation. The notion of meaning here has two distinct senses: meaning of the content of a set of symbols, and the meaning inferred by the analyst from any pattern of similarities and differences in a domain of material remains.

Archaeological interpretation, like ethnographic interpretation, requires the selection of significant variation. As in ethnography, this selection derives its support from the coherence of distinct dimensions of variation, made mutually intelligible by the proposed interpretation (Hodder 1986 : 135−136). The final result is the construction of a written account of "projected contemporary thought about past actuality integrated and synthesized into contexts in terms of culture, sequential time, and contemporary values and interests" (Deetz 1988 : 15, following Taylor 1948 : 34−35).

Since archaeologists are constructing, not simply reconstructing, the past, "the study of prehistory must be essentially an *explanation* of the archaeological record" (Trigger 1978 : 52; emphasis added). Each such explanation is only one of several possible. But because the archaeological record is the only primary source of data for the explanation of past actuality, it must be used to address that issue:

> Under these circumstances, the elucidation of historical events
> inevitably assumes the form of a "how possibly" rather than a

"why necessarily" explanation. . . . An important characteristic of "how possibly" explanations is the reconstruction of a chain of events, accompanied by an effort to account for these events and their sequence . . .

By providing new evidence about the event, or series of events, the archaeological record offers a test of the adequacy of the reconstruction, and also of the interpretation, of the event. This is inevitable because, in explaining the evidence, certain tentative hypotheses will have been advanced concerning aspects of what happened not covered by the archaeological evidence that originally was available . . . This mode of explanation also attaches special significance to the archaeological record. Instead of being seen as only another source of data for generalizing about cultural processes, the archaeological record becomes the most important means by which the prehistory of [humanity] can be reconstructed and explained . . . it becomes both expedient and reasonable to view the primary aim of archaeology as being the explanation of the archaeological record rather than the nature of material culture. (Trigger 1978:48)

This is the goal toward which I have worked in this archaeological ethnography: the explanation of the archaeological record available at this point in time. The adequacy of this explanation, shaped as it is by a particular set of concerns and necessarily based on a selective consideration of material remains, may be partially judged by the coherence of this particular interpretation. Since the understanding of Cerro Palenque suggested in the preceding chapters has implications beyond the original data, continued research in Honduras and greater Mesoamerica will also refine and perhaps lead to the rejection of some or all of this interpretation. Accepting the task of archaeology as the construction of a representation of a past actuality necessarily brings with it such risks, but there is no substitute for this primary goal of archaeology as anthropology.

I also realize that other observers might construct distinctive interpretations. James Clifford (1988:38) suggests the metaphor of reading a text for cultural interpretation, implying that there will be many possible readings of the same text. Christopher Tilley (1989) suggests viewing archaeological interpretation as akin to drama, in which the play may be the same, but performances differ. The role of the author, using this metaphor, is similar to that of the director of a dramatic performance. Readers, like critics in the theater, are free to evaluate the adequacy of this performance, and other directors to make use of the script.

References Cited

Adams, Richard Newbold

1957 *Cultural Surveys of Panama, Nicaragua, Guatemala, El Salvador, Honduras.* Pan-American Sanitary Bureau Publication 33. Washington, D.C.

1975 *Energy and Structure: A Theory of Social Power.* Austin: University of Texas Press.

1989 The Conquest Tradition of Mesoamerica. *The Americas: A Quarterly Review of Inter-American Cultural History* 46(2): 119–136.

Agurcia Fasquelle, Ricardo

1978 Las figurillas de Playa de los Muertos, Honduras. *Yaxkin* 2(4): 221–240.

1980 Asentamientos del Clásico Tardío en el valle de Comayagua. *Yaxkin* 3(4): 249–264.

1986 Late Classic Settlements in the Comayagua Valley. In *The Southeast Maya Periphery,* edited by Patricia A. Urban and Edward M. Schortman, pp. 262–274. Austin: University of Texas Press.

Andrews IV, E. Wyllys

1969 *The Archaeological Use and Distribution of Mollusca in the Maya Lowlands.* Middle American Research Institute Publication 34. New Orleans: Tulane University.

Andrews V, E. Wyllys

1976 *The Archaeology of Quelepa, El Salvador.* Middle American Research Institute Publication 42. New Orleans: Tulane University.

Appleby, Gordon

1976 Export Monoculture and Regional Social Structure in Puno, Peru. In *Regional Analysis,* vol. 2, *Social Systems,* edited by Carol A. Smith, pp. 291–307. New York: Academic Press.

Ashmore, Wendy

1981 Some Issues of Method and Theory in Lowland Maya Settlement Archaeology. In *Lowland Maya Settlement Patterns,* edited by Wendy Ashmore, pp. 37–69. Albuquerque: University of New Mexico Press.

1986 Peten Cosmology in the Maya Southeast: An Analysis of Architecture and Settlement Patterns at Classic Quirigua. In *The South-*

east Maya Periphery, edited by Patricia A. Urban and Edward M. Schortman, pp. 35–49. Austin: University of Texas Press.

1987   Cobble Crossroads: Gualjoquito Architecture and External Elite Ties. In *Interaction on the Southeast Mesoamerican Frontier: Prehistoric and Historic Honduras and El Salvador,* edited by Eugenia J. Robinson. BAR International Series 327(i): 28–48. Oxford.

1988   Proyecto Arqueológico Copan de Cosmología/Copán North Group Project, June–July 1988. Preliminary Report to the Instituto Hondureño de Antropología e Historia and the National Geographic Society.

1989   Construction and Cosmology: Politics and Ideology in Lowland Maya Settlement Patterns. In *Word and Image in Maya Culture: Explorations in Language, Writing, and Representation,* edited by William F. Hanks and Donald S. Rice, pp. 272–286. Salt Lake City: University of Utah Press.

Bailey, Kenneth

1973   Monothetic and Polythetic Typologies and Their Relation to Conceptualization, Measurement and Scaling. *American Sociological Review* 38: 18–33.

Baudez, Claude

1966   Niveaux céramiques au Honduras: Une Reconsidération de l'évolution culturelle. *Journal de la Société des Américanistes de Paris* 55: 299–341.

Baudez, Claude, and Pierre Becquelin

1973   *Archéologie de los Naranjos, Honduras.* Etudes Mésoaméricaines 2. Mexico City: Mission Archéologique et Ethnologique Française au Mexique.

Beaudry, Marilyn P.

1984   *Ceramic Production and Distribution in the Southeastern Maya Periphery: Late Classic Painted Serving Vessels.* BAR International Series 203. Oxford.

Beaudry, Marilyn P., Rosemary A. Joyce, and Eugenia J. Robinson.

n.d.   Classic Period Ceramic Complexes of the Ulua Valley. To be published in *Ceramics of Precolumbian Honduras,* edited by Marilyn P. Beaudry and John Henderson.

Benyo, Julie C.

1986   An Archaeological Investigation of Intra-Community Social Organization at La Ceiba, Comayagua, Honduras. Doctoral dissertation, Department of Anthropology, State University of New York at Albany.

Bergmann, John

1969   The Distribution of Cacao Cultivation in Pre-Columbian America. *Annals of the Association of American Geographers* 59(1): 85–96.

Bonsack Kelley, Klara

1976   Dendritic Central-Place Systems and the Regional Organization of Navajo Trading Posts. In *Regional Analysis,* vol. 1, *Economic Sys-*

tems, edited by Carol A. Smith, pp. 219–254. New York: Academic Press.

Borhegyi, Stephan F. de
1969 The Pre-Columbian Ballgame—A Pan-Mesoamerican Tradition. 38th International Congress of Americanists (1968), *Proceedings* 1:499–515. Stuttgart-Munich.

Bullard, William
1964 Settlement Pattern and Social Structure in the Southern Maya Lowlands during the Classic Period. In *Actas y Memorias del XXXV Congreso Internacional de Americanistas* 1:279–287. Mexico City.

Calnek, Edward
1976 The Internal Structure of Tenochtitlan. In *The Valley of Mexico,* edited by Eric R. Wolf, pp. 287–302. Albuquerque: University of New Mexico Press.

Campbell, Lyle
1976 The Linguistic Prehistory of the Southern Mesoamerican Periphery. In *Las fronteras de Mesoamérica.* Sociedad Mexicana de Antropología, Mesa Redonda 14(1):157–183. Tegucigalpa.
1979 Middle American Languages. In *The Languages of Native America,* edited by Lyle Campbell and Marianne Mithun, pp. 902–1000. Austin: University of Texas Press.

Campbell, Lyle, and Terrence Kaufman
1976 A Linguistic Look at the Olmecs. *American Antiquity* 41(1):80–89.

Canby, Joel
1949 Excavations at Yarumela, Spanish Honduras. Doctoral dissertation, Department of Anthropology, Harvard University.
1951 Possible Chronological Implications of the Long Ceramic Sequence Recovered at Yarumela, Spanish Honduras. In *The Civilizations of Ancient America: Selected Papers of the 29th International Congress of Americanists,* vol. 1, edited by Sol Tax, pp. 79–92. New York: Cooper Square Publishers.

Cancian, Frank
1965 *Economics and Prestige in a Maya Community: The Religious Cargo System in Zinacantan.* Stanford: Stanford University Press.

Castegnaro de Foletti, Alessandra
1989 *Alfarería Lenca contemporánea de Honduras.* [Tegucigalpa?]: Editorial Guaymuras.

Chamberlain, Robert S.
1953 *The Conquest and Colonization of Honduras, 1502–1550.* Carnegie Institution of Washington Publication 598. Washington, D.C.

Chapman, Anne
1978 *Los lencas de Honduras en el siglo XVI.* Estudios Antropológicos e Históricos No. 2. Tegucigalpa: Instituto Hondureño de Antropología e Historia.
1985 *Los hijos del copal y la candela,* vol. 1, *Ritos agrarios y tradición*

oral de los lencas de Honduras. Serie Antropológica 64. Mexico
City: Universidad Nacional Antónoma de México, Instituto de Investigaciones Antropológicas.

1986   *Los hijos del copal y la candela,* vol. 2, *Tradición católica de los
lencas de Honduras.* Serie Antropológica 86. Mexico City: Universidad Nacional Autónoma de México, Instituto de Investigaciones
Antropológicas.

Chase, Diane
1986   Social and Political Organization in the Land of Cacao and Honey:
Correlating the Archaeology and Ethnohistory of the Postclassic
Lowland Maya. In *Late Lowland Maya Civilization,* edited by
Jeremy A. Sabloff and E. Wyllys Andrews V, pp. 347–378. Albu-
querque: University of New Mexico Press.

Clifford, James
1986   Introduction: Partial Truths. In *Writing Culture: The Poetics and
Politics of Ethnography,* edited by James Clifford and George Marcus, pp. 1–26. Berkeley: University of California Press.

1988   *The Predicament of Culture: Twentieth Century Ethnography,
Literature and Art.* Cambridge, Mass.: Harvard University Press.

Clifford, James, and George E. Marcus
1986   *Writing Culture: The Poetics and Politics of Ethnography.* Berkeley:
University of California Press.

Coe, Michael D.
1965   The Olmec Style and Its Distributions. In *Handbook of Middle
American Indians* 3:739–775. Edited by Robert Wauchope and
Gordon R. Willey. Austin: University of Texas Press.

Coe, Michael D., and Richard A. Diehl
1980   *In the Land of the Olmec,* vol. 2, *The People of the River.* Austin:
University of Texas Press.

Coggins, Clemency
1988   On the Historical Significance of Decorated Ceramics at Copan
and Quirigua and Related Classic Maya Sites. In *The Southeast
Classic Maya Zone,* edited by Elizabeth H. Boone and Gordon R.
Willey, pp. 95–124. Washington, D.C.: Dumbarton Oaks.

Deetz, James
1988   History and Archaeological Theory: Walter Taylor Revisited.
American Antiquity 53(1):13–22.

Demarest, Arthur A.
1986   *The Archaeology of Santa Leticia and the Rise of Maya Civilization.* Middle American Research Institute Publication 52. New Orleans: Tulane University.

Demarest, Arthur A., and Robert J. Sharer
1982   The Origins and Evolution of the Usulutan Ceramic Style. *American Antiquity* 47:810–822.

1986   Late Preclassic Ceramic Spheres, Culture Areas, and Cultural Evolution in the Southeastern Highlands of Mesoamerica. In *The*

Southeast Maya Periphery, edited by Patricia A. Urban and Edward M. Schortman, pp. 194–223. Austin: University of Texas Press.

Denevan, William
1982 Hydraulic Agriculture in the American Tropics: Forms, Measures, and Recent Research. In *Maya Subsistence,* edited by Kent V. Flannery, pp. 181–203. New York: Academic Press.

Dixon, Boyd M.
1987 Conflict along the Southeast Mesoamerican Periphery: A Defensive Wall System at the Site of Tenampua. In *Interaction on the Southeast Mesoamerican Frontier: Prehistoric and Historic Honduras and El Salvador,* edited by Eugenia J. Robinson. BAR International Series 327(i): 142–153. Oxford.

1989 A Preliminary Settlement Pattern Study of a Prehistoric Cultural Corridor: The Comayagua Valley, Honduras. *Journal of Field Archaeology* 16(3): 257–272.

Elvir A., Reniery
1974 *Mapa geológico de la República de Honduras, primera edición,* 1:500,000. Tegucigalpa: Instituto Geográfico Nacional de Honduras.

Epstein, Jeremiah
1957 Late Ceramic Horizons in Northeastern Honduras. Doctoral dissertation, Department of Anthropology, University of Pennsylvania. Ann Arbor: University Microfilms.

1959 Dating the Ulua Polychrome Complex. *American Antiquity* 25:125–129.

Erasmus, Charles
1968 Thoughts on Upward Collapse: An Essay on Explanation in Anthropology. *Southwest Journal of Anthropology* 24(2):170–194.

Fash, William L., Jr.
1983a Deducing Social Organization from Classic Maya Settlement Patterns: A Case Study from the Copan Valley. In *Civilization in the Ancient Americas,* edited by Richard M. Leventhal and Alan L. Kolata, pp. 261–288. Albuquerque and Cambridge, Mass.: University of New Mexico Press and Peabody Museum of Archaeology and Ethnology, Harvard University.

1983b Maya State Formation: A Case Study and Its Implications. Doctoral dissertation, Department of Anthropology, Harvard University.

1985 La secuencia de ocupación del grupo 9N-8, Las Sepulturas, Copán, y sus implicaciones teóricas. *Yaxkin* 8 (1–2): 135–150.

1986a History and Characteristics of Settlement in the Copan Valley, and Some Comparisons with Quirigua. In *The Southeast Maya Periphery,* edited by Patricia A. Urban and Edward M. Schortman, pp. 72–93. Austin: University of Texas Press.

1986b La fachada esculpida de la estructura 9N-82: Composición, forma e iconografía. In *Proyecto Arqueológico Copán Segunda Fase: Excavaciones en el area urbana de Copán,* vol. 1, edited by William T. Sanders, pp. 319–342. Tegucigalpa: SECTUR.

Fash, William L. Jr., and Sherree Lane
   1983   El juego de pelota B. In *Introducción a la arqueología de Copán,
          Honduras,* vol. 2, edited by Claude Baudez, pp. 501–562. Tegu-
          cigalpa: SECTUR.
Feldman, Lawrence H.
   1974   Shells from Afar: 'Panamic' Molluscs in Mayan Sites. In *Meso-
          american Archaeology: New Approaches,* edited by Norman Ham-
          mond, pp. 129–133. Austin: University of Texas Press.
   1975   *Riverine Maya: The Torquegua and Other Chols of the Lower
          Motagua Valley.* University of Missouri-Columbia, Museum of
          Anthropology, Museum Briefs No. 15.
Firth, Raymond
   1963   *Elements of Social Organization.* Boston: Beacon Press.
Flannery, Kent V.
   1968   The Olmec and the Valley of Oaxaca: A Model for Inter-regional
          Interaction in Formative Times. In *Dumbarton Oaks Conference
          on the Olmec,* edited by Elizabeth P. Benson, pp. 79–118. Washing-
          ton, D.C.: Dumbarton Oaks.
Foster, George
   1967   *Tzintzuntzan: Mexican Peasants in a Changing World.* Boston:
          Little, Brown and Company.
Freidel, David
   1979   Culture Areas and Interaction Spheres: Contrasting Approaches to
          the Emergence of Civilization in the Maya Lowlands. *American
          Antiquity* 44:36–55.
Geertz, Clifford
   1973   Thick Description: Toward an Interpretive Theory of Culture. In
          The Interpretation of Cultures, pp. 3–31. New York: Basic Books.
   1980   *Negara: The Theatre State in Nineteenth-Century Bali.* Princeton:
          Princeton University Press.
Gerstle, Andrea
   1985   La arquitectura ceremonial de Las Sepulturas, Copán. *Yaxkin*
          8(1–2):99–110.
Gillespie, Susan
   1985   Ballgames and Boundaries. Paper presented at the International
          Symposium on the Mesoamerican Ballgame and Ballcourts, Tucson.
Glass, John B.
   1966   Archaeological Survey of Western Honduras. In *Handbook of
          Middle American Indians* 4:157–179. Edited by Robert Wau-
          chope, Gordon F. Ekholm, and Gordon R. Willey. Austin: Univer-
          sity of Texas Press.
Gordon, George Byron
   1896   *Prehistoric Ruins of Copan, Honduras: A Preliminary Report of
          the Explorations by the Museum, 1891–1896.* Peabody Museum
          Memoirs 1(1). Cambridge, Mass.
   1898a *Caverns of Copan, Honduras.* Peabody Museum Memoirs 1(5).
          Cambridge, Mass.

1898b *Researches in the Uloa Valley, Honduras.* Peabody Museum Memoirs 1(4). Cambridge, Mass.
1902 *The Hieroglyphic Stairway, Ruins of Copan.* Peabody Museum Memoirs 1(6). Cambridge, Mass.

Grove, David C.
1981 The Formative Period and the Evolution of Complex Culture. *Handbook of Middle American Indians, Supplement* 1 : 373 – 391. Edited by Victoria Reifler Bricker and Jeremy A. Sabloff. Austin: University of Texas Press.

Hammond, Norman
1972 Obsidian Trade Routes in the Maya Area. *Science* 178 : 1092 – 1093.
1976 Maya Obsidian Trade in Southern Belize. In *Maya Lithic Studies,* edited by Thomas R. Hester and Norman Hammond, pp. 71 – 81. Center for Archaeological Research, University of Texas at San Antonio, Special Report No. 4. San Antonio.

Hasemann, George
1985 Desarrollo de los asentamientos Clásicos Tardíos a lo largo del Río Sulaco. *Yaxkin* 8(1 – 2): 25 – 46.
1987 Late Classic Settlement on the Sulaco River, Central Honduras. In *Chiefdoms in the Americas,* edited by Robert D. Drennan and Carlos A. Uribe, pp. 85 – 103. Lanham, Md.: University Press of America.

Hasemann, George, Boyd Dixon, and John Yonk
1982 El rescate arqueológico en la zona de embalse de El Cajón: Reconocimiento general y regional, 1980 – 1981. *Yaxkin* 5(1): 22 – 36.

Hasemann, George, Lori Van Gerpen, and Vito Veliz
1977 *Informe preliminar, Curruste: Fase 1.* San Pedro Sula: Patronato Pro-Curruste-Instituto Hondureño de Antropología e Historia.

Healy, Paul
1974 The Cuyamel Caves: Preclassic Sites in Northeast Honduras. *American Antiquity* 39 : 433 – 437.
1978a Excavations at Rio Claro (H-CN-12), Northeast Honduras: Preliminary Report. *Journal of Field Archaeology* 5 : 15 – 28.
1978b Excavations at Selin Farm (H-CN-5), Colon, Northeast Honduras. *Vínculos* 4 : 57 – 79. San José, Costa Rica.
1984 The Archaeology of Honduras. In *The Archaeology of Lower Central America,* edited by Frederick W. Lange and Doris Z. Stone, pp. 113 – 164. Albuquerque: University of New Mexico Press.
1988 Music of the Maya. *Archaeology* 41(1): 24 – 31.

Helms, Mary W.
1979 *Ancient Panama: Chiefs in Search of Power.* Austin: University of Texas Press.
1988 *Ulysses' Sail: An Ethnographic Odyssey of Power, Knowledge, and Geographical Distance.* Princeton: Princeton University Press.

Henderson, John S.
1978 El noroeste de Honduras y la frontera oriental Maya. *Yaxkin* 2(4): 241 – 254.

1979   The Valle de Naco: Ethnohistory and Archaeology in Northwestern Honduras. *Ethnohistory* 24(4):363–377.

1984   (ed.) *Archaeology in Northwestern Honduras: Interim Reports of the Proyecto Arqueológico Sula,* vol. 1. Ithaca: Latin American Studies Program–Archaeology Program, Cornell University.

Henderson, John S., Ilene Sterns, Anthony Wonderley, and Patricia A. Urban

1979   Archaeological Investigations in the Valle de Naco, Northwestern Honduras: A Preliminary Report. *Journal of Field Archaeology* 6:169–192.

Hendon, Julia

1987   The Uses of Maya Structures. Doctoral dissertation, Department of Anthropology, Harvard University. Ann Arbor: University Microfilms.

Henrickson, Elizabeth, and Mary McDonald

1983   Ceramic Form and Function: An Ethnographic Search and an Archaeological Application. *American Anthropologist* 85:630–643.

Hirth, Kenneth

1982   Excavaciones en Salitrón Viejo: 1981. *Yaxkin* 5(1):51–66.

1988   Beyond the Maya Frontier: Cultural Interaction and Syncretism along the Central Honduran Corridor. In *The Southeast Classic Maya Zone,* edited by Elizabeth H. Boone and Gordon R. Willey, pp. 297–334. Washington, D.C.: Dumbarton Oaks.

Hirth, Kenneth, Patricia A. Urban, George Hasemann, and Vito Veliz

1981   Patrones regionales de asentamiento en la región de El Cajon: Departamentos de Comayagua y Yoro, Honduras. *Yaxkin* 4:33–55.

Hodder, Ian

1986   *Reading the Past: Current Approaches to Interpretation in Archaeology.* New York: Cambridge University Press.

1989   Writing Archaeology: Site Reports in Context. *Antiquity* 63(239): 268–274.

Holt, Dennis, and William Bright

1976   La lengua paya y las fronteras lingüísticas de mesoamérica. In *Las fronteras de Mesoamérica.* Sociedad Mexicana de Antropología, Mesa Redonda 14(1):149–156. Tegucigalpa.

Joesink Mandeville, L. R. V.

1987   Yarumela, Honduras: Formative Period Cultural Conservatism and Diffusion. In *Interaction on the Southeast Mesoamerican Frontier: Prehistoric and Historic Honduras and El Salvador,* edited by Eugenia J. Robinson. BAR International Series 327(i):196–214. Oxford.

Johnson, Gregory

1977   Aspects of Regional Analysis in Archaeology. *Annual Reviews in Anthropology* 6:479–508. Palo Alto.

Joyce, Rosemary A.

1982   La zona arqueológica de Cerro Palenque. *Yaxkin* 5(2):95–101.

1983   Travesía (CR-35), Archaeological Investigations, 1983. Report submitted to the Instituto Hondureño de Antropología e Historia, Tegucigalpa.

1985 Cerro Palenque, Valle del Ulua, Honduras: Terminal Classic Interaction on the Southern Mesoamerican Periphery. Doctoral dissertation, Department of Anthropology, University of Illinois. Ann Arbor: University Microfilms.

1986 Terminal Classic Interaction on the Southeastern Maya Periphery. *American Antiquity* 51:313–329.

1987a Intraregional Ceramic Variation and Social Class: Developmental Trajectories of Classic Period Ceramic Complexes from the Ulua Valley. In *Interaction on the Southeast Mesoamerican Frontier: Prehistoric and Historic Honduras and El Salvador,* edited by Eugenia J. Robinson. BAR International Series 327(ii):280–303. Oxford.

1987b Patrón de asentamiento. Paper presented at the IV Seminario Sobre la Arqueología, Instituto Hondureño de Antropología e Historia, La Ceiba.

1987c The Terminal Classic Ceramics of Cerro Palenque, Honduras: A Southeastern Outlier of the Boca Ceramic Sphere. In *Maya Ceramics: Papers from the 1985 Maya Ceramic Conference,* edited by Prudence M. Rice and Robert J. Sharer 1:397–428. BAR International Series 345. Oxford.

1988a Ceramic Traditions and Language Groups of Prehispanic Honduras. *Journal of the Steward Anthropological Society* 15(1–2): 158–186.

1988b The Ulua Valley and the Coastal Maya Lowlands: The View from Cerro Palenque. In *The Southeast Classic Maya Zone,* edited by Elizabeth H. Boone and Gordon R. Willey, pp. 269–296. Washington, D.C.: Dumbarton Oaks.

1988c Ceramic Units of Terminal Classic Cerro Palenque, Honduras. *Cerámica de Cultura Maya et al.* 15:31–34.

n.d. Ulua Polychromes from the Peabody Museum. Ms. in the possession of the author.

Joyce, Rosemary A., Richard Edging, Karl Lorenz, and Susan Gillespie

1986 Olmec Bloodletting: An Iconographic Study. Paper presented at the Sixth Palenque Mesa Redonda. (In press, Norman: University of Oklahoma Press.)

Joyce, Rosemary A., and Russell Sheptak

1983 Settlement in the Southwest Hills and Central Alluvium, Valle de Ulua. Report submitted to Proyecto Arqueológico Sula, Instituto Hondureño de Antropología e Historia, Tegucigalpa.

1988 El Remolino (CR-260): Excavation and Analysis of a Protoclassic Ceramic Complex on the Río Chamelecón, 1987. Report submitted to the Proyecto Arqueológico Sula, Instituto Hondureño de Antropología e Historia, Tegucigalpa.

Joyce, Rosemary A., Russell Sheptak, Julia Hendon, Christopher Fung, and

John Gerry
   1989   Settlement Patterns in Yoro, Honduras. Paper presented in the session "Maya Settlement Patterns and Spatial Analysis" at the 88th Annual Meeting of the American Anthropological Association, Washington, D.C.
Kennedy, Nedenia
   1978   Acerca de la frontera en Playa de los Muertos, Honduras. *Yaxkin* 2(3):203–215.
   1980   La cronología cerámica del Formativo de Playa de Los Muertos, Honduras. *Yaxkin* 3(4):265–272.
   1981   The Formative Period Ceramic Sequence from Playa de los Muertos, Honduras. Doctoral dissertation, Department of Anthropology, University of Illinois. Ann Arbor: University Microfilms.
   1982a Continuación del análisis de la cerámica: La secuencia cerámica preliminar de Salitrón Viejo (PC1). In *Segundo informe trimestral, Proyecto Arqueológico El Cajón,* edited by Kenneth Hirth, Gloria Lara, and George Hasemann, pp. 24–36. Tegucigalpa: Instituto Hondureño de Antropología e Historia.
   1982b Un resúmen de la secuencia formativa de Playa de los Muertos, Honduras. *Yaxkin* 5(2):110–118.
Kidder, Alfred V.
   1947   *The Artifacts of Uaxactun, Guatemala.* Carnegie Institution of Washington Publication 576. Washington, D.C.
Kirchhoff, Paul
   1952   Mesoamerica: Its Geographic Limits, Ethnic Composition and Cultural Characteristics. In *Heritage of Conquest,* edited by Sol Tax, pp. 17–30. New York: Macmillan Company.
Klein, Cecelia
   1987   The Ideology of Autosacrifice at the Templo Mayor. In *The Aztec Templo Mayor,* edited by Elizabeth H. Boone, pp. 293–370. Washington, D.C.: Dumbarton Oaks.
Lamberg-Karlovsky, C. C.
   1989   Introduction. In *Archaeological Thought in America,* edited by C. C. Lamberg-Karlovsky, pp. 1–16. Cambridge: Cambridge University Press.
Landa, Diego de
   1973   *Relación de las cosas de Yucatán.* Mexico City: Editorial Porrúa.
Lange, Fred
   1984   The Greater Nicoya Archaeological Subarea. In *The Archaeology of Lower Central America,* edited by Frederick W. Lange and Doris Z. Stone, pp. 165–194. Albuquerque: University of New Mexico Press.
Lara Pinto, Gloria
   1982   Beitrage zur indianischen Ethnographie von Honduras in der ersten Hälfte des 16. Jahrhunderts, unter besonderer Berucksichtigung der Historischen Demographie. Doctoral dissertation, University of Hamburg, Germany.

Lara Pinto, Gloria, and Russell Sheptak
  1985 Excavaciones en el sitio de Intendencia, Río Humuya: Primeros resultados. *Yaxkin* 8(1–2):13–24.
Leventhal, Richard M.
  1979 Settlement Patterns at Copán, Honduras. Doctoral dissertation, Department of Anthropology, Harvard University.
  1983 Household Groups and Classic Maya Religion. In *Prehistoric Settlement Patterns: Essays in Honor of Gordon R. Willey,* edited by Evon Z. Vogt and Richard M. Leventhal, pp. 55–76. Albuquerque and Cambridge, Mass.: University of New Mexico Press and the Peabody Museum, Harvard University.
Lévi-Strauss, Claude
  1976 Relations of Symmetry between Rituals and Myths of Neighboring Peoples. In *Structural Anthropology,* vol. 2, translated by Monique Layton, pp. 238–255. Chicago: University of Chicago Press.
Lincoln, Charles
  1979 Architectural Test Excavations at Travesía, Honduras. *Human Mosaic* 13:15–24. New Orleans.
  1986 The Chronology of Chichen Itza: A Review of the Literature. In *Late Lowland Maya Civilization: Classic to Postclassic,* edited by Jeremy A. Sabloff and E. Wyllys Andrews V, pp. 141–196. Albuquerque: University of New Mexico Press.
Longyear, John M.
  1947 *Cultures and Peoples of the Southeastern Maya Frontier.* Carnegie Institution of Washington, Theoretical Approaches to Problems Series 3. Cambridge, Mass.
  1952 *Copan Ceramics: A Study of Southeastern Maya Pottery.* Carnegie Institution of Washington Publication 597. Washington, D.C.
Lothrop, Samuel K.
  1924 *Tulum: An Archaeological Study of the East Coast of Yucatan.* Carnegie Institution of Washington Publication 335. Washington, D.C.
  1927 The Museum Central American Expedition, 1925–1926. *Indian Notes* 4:12–33. New York: Museum of the American Indian, Heye Foundation.
  1939 The Southeastern Frontier of the Maya. *American Anthropologist* 41:42–54.
Lounsbury, Floyd G.
  1985 The Identities of the Mythological Figures in the Cross Group Inscriptions of Palenque. In *Fourth Palenque Round Table, 1980,* edited by Merle Greene Robertson and Elizabeth P. Benson, pp. 45–58. San Francisco: Pre-Columbian Art Research Institute.
Lowe, Gareth
  1981 Olmec Horizons Defined in Mound 20, San Isidro, Chiapas. In *The Olmec and Their Neighbors,* edited by Elizabeth P. Benson, pp. 231–256. Washington, D.C.: Dumbarton Oaks.
Mallory, John
  1984 Late Classic Maya Economic Specialization: Evidence from the

Copan Obsidian Assemblage. Doctoral dissertation, Department of Anthropology, Pennsylvania State University. Ann Arbor: University Microfilms.

Marcus, George E., and Michael M. J. Fischer

1986 *Anthropology as Cultural Critique: An Experimental Moment in the Human Sciences.* Chicago: University of Chicago Press.

Marcus, Joyce

1976 *Emblem and State in the Classic Maya Lowlands.* Washington, D.C.: Dumbarton Oaks.

1978 Archaeology and Religion: A Comparison of the Zapotec and Maya. *World Archaeology* 10(2): 172–191.

Maschner, Herbert

1982 Un análisis lítico comparativo de la Guacamaya y El Bálsamo: Dos centros mayores al sureste del valle de Sula. *Yaxkin* 5(2): 106–109.

Mathews, Peter

1980 Notes on the Dynastic Sequence of Bonampak, Part 1. In *Third Palenque Round Table, 1978, Part 2,* edited by Merle Greene Robertson, pp. 60–73. Austin: University of Texas Press.

Maudslay, Alfred P.

1889–1902 *Biologia centrali-americana: Archaeology.* London: R. H. Porter and Dulan and Co.

Miller, Arthur G.

1982 *On the Edge of the Sea: Mural Painting at Tancah-Tulum, Quintana Roo, Mexico.* Washington, D.C.: Dumbarton Oaks.

Miller, Mary Ellen, and Stephen Houston

1987 The Classic Maya Ballgame and Its Architectural Setting: A Study of Relations between Text and Image. *Res* 14: 47–66.

Millon, René

1955 When Money Grew on Trees: A Study of Cacao in Ancient Mesoamerica. Doctoral dissertation, Department of Anthropology, Columbia University.

1974 The Study of Urbanism at Teotihuacan, Mexico. In *Mesoamerican Archaeology: New Approaches,* edited by Norman Hammond, pp. 335–362. Austin: University of Texas Press.

1981 Teotihuacan: City, State, and Civilization. In *Handbook of Middle American Indians, Supplement* 1: 198–243. Edited by Victoria Reifler Bricker and Jeremy A. Sabloff. Austin: University of Texas Press.

Moholy-Nagy, Hattula

1976 Spatial Distribution of Flint and Obsidian Artifacts at Tikal, Guatemala. In *Maya Lithic Studies,* edited by Thomas R. Hester and Norman Hammond, pp. 91–108. Center for Archaeological Research, University of Texas at San Antonio, Special Report No. 4. San Antonio.

Pendergast, David

1967 Ocupación Post-Clásica en Altun Ha, Honduras Británica. *Revista Mexicana de Estudios Antropológicos* 21: 213–224.

1971 Evidence of Early Teotihuacan–Lowland Maya Contact at Altun Ha. *American Antiquity* 36(4):455–460.

1986 Stability through Change: Lamanai, Belize, from the Ninth to the Seventeenth Century. In *Late Lowland Maya Civilization: Classic to Postclassic*, edited by Jeremy A. Sabloff and E. Wyllys Andrews V, pp. 223–249. Albuquerque: University of New Mexico Press.

Polanyi, Karl
1958 The Economy as Instituted Process. In *Trade and Market in the Early Empires*, edited by Karl Polanyi, Conrad M. Arensberg, and Harry W. Pearson, pp. 243–270. Glencoe, Ill.: Free Press.

Pollock, H. E. D.
1980 *The Puuc: An Architectural Survey of the Hill Country of Yucatan and Northern Campeche, Mexico.* Harvard University, Peabody Museum of Archaeology and Ethnology, Memoir 19. Cambridge, Mass.

Pollock, H. E. D., Ralph L. Roys, Tatiana Proskouriakoff, and A. Ledyard Smith
1962 *Mayapan, Yucatan, Mexico.* Carnegie Institution of Washington Publication 619. Washington, D.C.

Pope, Kevin O.
1984 The Recent Geologic History of the Sula Valley. In *Archaeology in Northwestern Honduras: Interim Reports of the Proyecto Arqueológico Sula*, vol. 1, edited by John S. Henderson, pp. 80–93. Ithaca: Archaeology Program–Latin American Studies Program, Cornell University.

1985 Palaeoecology of the Ulua Valley, Honduras: An Archaeological Perspective. Doctoral dissertation, Stanford University.

1987 The Ecology and Economy of the Formative-Classic Transition along the Ulua River, Honduras. In *Interaction on the Southeast Mesoamerican Frontier: Prehistoric and Historic Honduras and El Salvador*, edited by Eugenia J. Robinson. BAR International Series 327(i):95–128. Oxford.

Popenoe, Dorothy
1934 Some Excavations at Playa de los Muertos, Ulua River, Honduras. *Maya Research* 1:62–86.

1936 The Ruins of Tenampua, Honduras. *Smithsonian Institution Annual Report, 1935,* pp. 559–572. Washington, D.C.

Porter, Muriel N.
1953 *Tlatilco and the Pre-Classic Cultures of the New World.* Viking Fund Publications in Anthropology 19. New York: Wenner-Gren Foundation.

Price, Barbara J.
1974 The Burden of the *Cargo:* Ethnographical Models and Archaeological Inference. In *Mesoamerican Archaeology: New Approaches*, edited by Norman Hammond, pp. 445–465. Austin: University of Texas Press.

Quirarte, Jacinto
    1977   The Ballcourt in Mesoamerica: Its Architectural Development. In
        Pre-Columbian Art History, edited by Alana Cordy-Collins and
        J. Stern, pp. 191–212. Palo Alto: Peek Publications.
Rands, Robert
    1955   Some Manifestations of Water in Mesoamerican Art. Bureau of
        American Ethnology Bulletin 157. *Anthropological Papers* 48:
        265–394. Washington, D.C.
Reina, Ruben E., and Robert M. Hill II
    1978   *The Traditional Pottery of Guatemala*. Austin: University of Texas
        Press.
Riese, Berthold, and Claude Baudez
    1983   Esculturas de las Estructuras 10L-2 y 4. In *Introducción a la Ar-
        queología de Copán, Honduras*, vol. 2, edited by Claude Baudez,
        pp. 143–190. Tegucigalpa: SECTUR.
Robinson, Eugenia J.
    1978   Maya Design Features of Mayoid Vessels of the Ulua-Yojoa Poly-
        chromes. Master's thesis, Department of Anthropology, Tulane
        University.
    1982   El patrón de asentamiento del sitio Guacamaya. *Yaxkin* 5(2):
        102–105.
    1983   The Prehistoric Colonization of the Alluvial Fans of the Southeast
        Side of the Sula Valley: An Interpretation of Process and Pattern.
        Report submitted to the Proyecto Arqueológico Sula, Instituto de
        Antropología e Historia.
    1986   A Typological Study of Prehistoric Settlement of the Eastern Al-
        luvial Fans, Sula Valley, Honduras: Comparison to Maya Settle-
        ment Forms. In *The Southeast Maya Periphery*, edited by Patricia
        A. Urban and Edward M. Schortman, pp. 239–261. Austin: Univer-
        sity of Texas Press.
    1987   Sula Valley Diachronic Regional and Interregional Interaction: A
        View from the East Side Alluvial Fans. In *Interaction on the South-
        east Mesoamerican Frontier: Prehistoric and Historic Honduras
        and El Salvador*, edited by Eugenia J. Robinson. BAR International
        Series 327(i): 154–195. Oxford.
    1988   Ceramic Spheres of the Southwest Mesoamerican Frontier. *Ce-
        rámica de Cultura Maya et al.* 15: 11–30. Philadelphia.
    1989   The Prehistoric Communities of the Sula Valley, Honduras: Re-
        gional Interaction in the Southeast Mesoamerican Frontier. Doc-
        toral dissertation, Department of Anthropology, Tulane University.
        Ann Arbor: University Microfilms.
Robinson, Eugenia J., George Hasemann, and Vito Veliz
    1979   An Archaeological Evaluation of Travesía, Honduras. *Human Mo-
        saic* 13: 1–14. New Orleans.
Robinson, Kenneth, Scott O'Mack, and William Loker
    1985   Excavaciones en la Plaza Principal del Conjunto Residencial Oeste
        de Salitrón Viejo (PC1). *Yaxkin* 8(1–2): 47–58.

Rouse, Irving
1960 The Classification of Artifacts in Archaeology. *American Antiquity* 25 : 313–323.
Rovner, Irwin
1975 Lithic Sequences from the Maya Lowlands. Doctoral dissertation, Department of Anthropology, University of Wisconsin, Madison.
1976 Pre-Columbian Maya Development of Utilitarian Lithic Industries: The Broad Perspective from Yucatan. In *Maya Lithic Studies*, edited by Thomas R. Hester and Norman Hammond, pp. 41–53. Center for Archaeological Research, University of Texas at San Antonio, Special Report No. 4. San Antonio.
Sabloff, Jeremy A.
1973 Continuity and Disruption during Terminal Late Classic Times at Seibal: Ceramics and Other Evidence. In *The Classic Maya Collapse*, edited by T. Patrick Culbert, pp. 107–131. Albuquerque: University of New Mexico Press.
1975 *Excavations at Seibal: Ceramics*. Harvard University Peabody Museum of Archaeology and Ethnology Memoirs 13 (2). Cambridge, Mass.
Sabloff, Jeremy A., and Gordon R. Willey
1967 The Collapse of Maya Civilization in the Southern Lowlands: A Consideration of History and Process. *Southwest Journal of Anthropology* 23(4) : 311–336.
Schele, Linda, and Mary Ellen Miller
1986 *The Blood of Kings: Dynasty and Ritual in Maya Art*. Fort Worth: Kimball Art Museum.
Schortman, Edward M., Patricia A. Urban, and Wendy Ashmore
1983 Santa Barbara Archaeological Project 1983 Season. A report prepared for the Instituto Hondureño de Antropología e Historia, Tegucigalpa.
Schortman, Edward M., Patricia A. Urban, Wendy Ashmore, and Julie Benyo
1986 Interregional Interaction in the Southeast Maya Periphery: The Santa Barbara Archaeological Project 1983–1984 Seasons. *Journal of Field Archaeology* 13 : 259–272.
Schwimmer, Brian
1976 Periodic Markets and Urban Development in Southern Ghana. In *Regional Analysis*, vol. 1, *Economic Systems*, edited by Carol A. Smith, pp. 123–146. New York: Academic Press.
Sharer, Robert J.
1978 *The Prehistory of Chalchuapa, El Salvador*. 3 vols. Philadelphia: University of Pennsylvania Press.
1980 The Quirigua Project, 1974–1979. *Expedition* 23(1) : 5–10.
Sheehy, James
1976 Preclassic Artifacts from Choloma, Cortés, Honduras. In *Las fronteras de Mesoamérica*. Sociedad Mexicana de Antropología, Mesa Redonda 14 (1) : 221–228.

1978 Informe preliminar sobre las excavaciones en Travesía en 1976. *Yaxkin* 2(3): 175−202.

1979 Ceramics from Colonia CARE (Choloma), Cortes, Honduras. *Cerámica de cultura Maya et al.* 10(2): 37−62.

1982 Cerámica pasta fina de Travesía. *Yaxkin* 5(2): 119−127.

Sheehy, James, and Vito Veliz

1977 Excavaciones recientes en Travesía, Valle de Sula. *Yaxkin* 2(2): 121−124.

Sheets, Payson D.

1972 A Model of Mesoamerican Obsidian Technology Based on Preclassic Workshop Debris in El Salvador. *Cerámica de Cultura Maya et al.* 8: 17−33. Philadelphia.

Sheptak, Russell N.

1982 Fotos aéreas y el patrón de asentamiento de la zona central del valle del Ulua. *Yaxkin* 5(2): 89−94.

1983 Geographic information in the *Repartimiento de San Pedro de Puerto de Caballos* (1536). Ms. in the possession of the author.

1985 Excavaciones de salvamento en Gualjoquito, Santa Barbara. *Yaxkin* 8(1−2): 191−206.

1987a Interaction between Belize and the Ulua Valley. In *Interaction on the Southeast Mesoamerican Frontier: Prehistoric and Historic Honduras and El Salvador*, edited by Eugenia J. Robinson. BAR International Series 327(ii): 247−266. Oxford.

1987b The Spanish *Entradas* into Northwestern Honduras. Paper presented at the Annual Meeting of the American Anthropological Association, Chicago.

Shook, Edwin

1954 The Temple of Kukulcan at Mayapan. Carnegie Institution of Washington, Department of Archaeology, *Current Reports* 2(20). Cambridge, Mass.

Shook, Edwin, and Tatiana Proskouriakoff

1956 Settlement Patterns in Mesoamerica and the Sequence in the Guatemalan Highlands. In *Prehistoric Settlement Patterns in the New World*, edited by Gordon R. Willey, pp. 93−100. Viking Fund Publications in Anthropology No. 23. New York: Wenner-Gren Foundation.

Smith, A. Ledyard

1961 Types of Ballcourts in the Highlands of Guatemala. In *Essays in Pre-Columbian Art and Archaeology*, edited by S. K. Lothrop et al., pp. 100−125. Cambridge, Mass.: Harvard University Press.

Smith, Carol A.

1976 Exchange Systems and the Spatial Distribution of Elites: The Organization of Stratification in Agrarian Societies. In *Regional Analysis*, vol. 2, *Social Systems*, edited by Carol A. Smith, pp. 309−374. New York: Academic Press.

Smith, M. F., Jr.

1985 Toward an Economic Interpretation of Ceramics: Relating Vessel

Size and Shape to Use. In *Decoding Prehistoric Ceramics,* edited by Ben A. Nelson, pp. 254–309. Carbondale: Southern Illinois University Press.

Smith, Robert E.

1971 *The Pottery of Mayapan.* Harvard University, Peabody Museum of Archaeology and Ethnology Papers 66. Cambridge, Mass.

Sorenson, Jerrel

1985 Observaciones preliminares sobre los artefactos líticos en el Valle del Río Sulaco. *Yaxkin* 8(1–2): 67–74.

Spaulding, Albert

1960 The Dimensions of Archaeology. In *Essays in the Science of Culture in Honor of Leslie A. White,* edited by Gertrude Evelyn Dole and Robert L. Carneiro, pp. 437–456. New York: Thomas Y. Crowell Co.

Squier, E. G.

1853 Ruins of Tenampua. Historical Society of New York *Proceedings,* pp. 1–8.

1870 *Honduras: Descriptive, Historical and Statistical.* London: Trubner and Co.

Stephens, John L.

1969 *Incidents of Travel in Central America, Chiapas and Yucatan.* 2 vols. New York: Dover Publications. Originally published in 1841.

Steward, Julian

1942 The Direct-Historical Approach to Archaeology. *American Antiquity* 7: 337–343.

Stone, Doris Z.

1940 The Ulua Valley and Lake Yojoa. In *The Maya and Their Neighbors,* edited by Clarence L. Hay, Ralph L. Linton, Samuel K. Lothrop, Harry L. Shapiro, and George C. Vaillant, pp. 386–394. New York: D. Appleton-Century.

1941 Archaeology of the North Coast of Honduras. *Peabody Museum Memoirs* 9(1). Cambridge.

1948 The Northern Highland Tribes: The Lenca. In *Handbook of South American Indians,* edited by Julian H. Steward 4: 205–217. Smithsonian Institution, Bureau of American Ethnology Bulletin 143. Washington, D.C.

1957 *The Archaeology of Southern and Central Honduras.* Peabody Museum of Archaeology and Ethnology Papers 49(3).

1969 Nahuat Traits in the Sula Plain, Northwestern Honduras. 38th International Congress of Americanists, *Proceedings* 1: 531–536. Stuttgart-Munich.

1970 An Interpretation of Ulua Polychrome Ware. 38th International Congress of Americanists (1968), *Proceedings* 2: 67–76. Stuttgart-Munich.

1972 *Pre-Columbian Man Finds Central America.* Cambridge, Mass.: Peabody Museum Press.

Strong, William Duncan

1948 The Archaeology of Honduras. In *Handbook of South American*

Indians, edited by Julian H. Steward 4:71–120. Smithsonian Institution, Bureau of American Ethnology Bulletin 143. Washington, D.C.

Strong, William Duncan, A. V. Kidder II, and A. J. Drexel Paul
1938   *Preliminary Report of the Smithsonian Institution–Harvard University Archaeological Expedition to Northwestern Honduras, 1936.* Smithsonian Institution Miscellaneous Collections 97. Washington, D.C.

Stross, Fred, Payson Sheets, Frank Asaro, and Helen Michel
1983   Precise Characterization of Guatemalan Obsidian Sources, and Source Determination of Artifacts from Quirigua. *American Antiquity* 48(2):323–336.

Taylor, Walter W.
1948   *A Study of Archeology.* American Anthropological Association Memoir 69. Washington, D.C.

Tedlock, Dennis
1985   *Popul Vuh: The Definitive Edition of the Mayan Book of the Dawn of Life and the Glories of the Gods and Kings.* New York: Simon and Schuster.

Thompson, J. Eric S.
1939   *Excavations at San Jose, British Honduras.* Carnegie Institution of Washington Publication 506. Washington, D.C.
1970   *Maya History and Religion.* Norman: University of Oklahoma Press.

Thompson, Raymond H.
1958   *Modern Yucatecan Maya Pottery Making.* Memoirs of the Society for American Archaeology No. 15. Salt Lake City.

Tilley, Christopher
1989   Excavation as Theatre. *Antiquity* 63(239):275–280.

Titulo de Yamala
n.d.   Titulo de Yamala (unpublished land title of Yamala, Departamento de Santa Barbara, Honduras). Ms. in the possession of the heirs of General Luis Bográn. Copy in the possession of the author.

Tolstoy, Paul
1971   Utilitarian Artifacts of Central Mexico. In *Handbook of Middle American Indians* 10(1):270–296. Edited by Robert Wauchope, Gordon F. Ekholm, and Ignacio Bernal. Austin: University of Texas Press.

Tourtellot, Gair
1983a Ancient Maya Settlements at Seibal, Peten, Guatemala: Peripheral Survey and Excavation. Doctoral dissertation, Department of Anthropology, Harvard University. Ann Arbor: University Microfilms.
1983b An Assessment of Classic Maya Household Composition. In *Prehistoric Settlement Patterns: Essays in Honor of Gordon R. Willey,* edited by Evon Z. Vogt and Richard M. Leventhal, pp. 35–54. Albuquerque and Cambridge, Mass.: University of New Mexico Press and the Peabody Museum, Harvard University.

1988 *Peripheral Survey and Excavation and Settlement and Community Patterns.* Excavations at Seibal, Department of Peten, Guatemala. Harvard University, Peabody Museum of Archaeology and Ethnology, Memoir 16. Cambridge, Mass.

Trigger, Bruce G.
1978 *Time and Traditions: Essays in Archaeological Interpretation.* New York: Columbia University Press.

Turner, Victor
1975 Symbolic Studies. *Annual Reviews in Anthropology* 4:145–161.

Urban, Patricia A.
1986a Systems of Precolumbian Settlement in the Naco Valley, Northwestern Honduras. Doctoral dissertation, Department of Anthropology, University of Pennsylvania. Ann Arbor: University Microfilms.
1986b Precolumbian Settlement in the Naco Valley, Northwestern Honduras. In *The Southeast Maya Periphery*, edited by Patricia A. Urban and Edward M. Schortman, pp. 275–295. Austin: University of Texas Press.

Urban, Patricia A., and Edward M. Schortman
1988 The Southeast Zone Viewed from the East: Lower Motagua-Naco Valleys. In *The Southeast Classic Maya Zone*, edited by Elizabeth H. Boone and Gordon R. Willey, pp. 223–268. Washington, D.C.: Dumbarton Oaks.

Vaillant, George C.
1927 The Chronological Significance of Maya Ceramics. Doctoral dissertation, Harvard University.
1934 The Archaeological Setting of the Playa de los Muertos Culture. *Maya Research* 1:87–100.

Viel, René
1978 Etude de la céramique Ulua-Yojoa Polychrome (nord-ouest de Honduras): Essai d'analyse stylistique du Babilonia. Doctoral dissertation, Université René Descartes, Paris.
1983 Evolución de la cerámica en Copán: Resultados preliminares. In *Introducción a la Arqueología de Copán, Honduras*, vol. 1, edited by Claude Baudez, pp. 473–549. Tegucigalpa: SECTUR.

Vlcek, David T., and William L. Fash, Jr.
1986 Survey in the Outlying Areas of the Copan Region, and the Copan-Quirigua "connection." In *The Southeast Maya Periphery*, edited by Patricia A. Urban and Edward M. Schortman, pp. 102–113. Austin: University of Texas Press.

Vogt, Evon Z.
1964 Some Implications of Zinacantan Social Structure for the Study of the Ancient Maya. In *Actas y Memorias del XXXV Congreso Internacional de Americanistas*, 1:307–319. Mexico City.
1969 *Zinacantan: A Maya Community in the Highlands of Chiapas.* Cambridge, Mass.: Belknap Press of Harvard University Press.

Walters, Gary Rex
 1980 The San Agustín Acasaguastlan Archaeological Project: The 1979
       Season. University of Missouri–Columbia, Museum of Anthropol-
       ogy, *Museum Briefs*, no. 25.
Watanabe, John
 1990 From Saints to Shibboleths: Image, Structure, and Identity in Maya
       Religious Syncretism. *American Ethnologist* 17(1):131–150.
Webster, David
 1977 Warfare and the Evolution of Maya Civilization. In *The Origins of
       Maya Civilization*, edited by Richard E. W. Adams, pp. 335–371.
       Albuquerque: University of New Mexico Press.
Webster, David, and AnnCorinne Freter
 1990 Settlement History and the Classic Collapse at Copan: A Re-
       defined Chronological Perspective. *Latin American Antiquity*
       1(1):66–85.
Weeks, John M., Nancy Black, and J. Stuart Speaker
 1987 From Prehistory to History in Western Honduras: The Care Lenca
       in the Colonial Province of Tencoa. In *Interaction on the Southeast
       Mesoamerican Frontier: Prehistoric and Historic Honduras and El
       Salvador*, edited by Eugenia J. Robinson. BAR International Series
       327(i):65–94. Oxford.
Whittington, Stephen
 1989 El Proyecto Ostumán: Resultados preliminares de las excavaciones.
       A paper presented at the V Seminario de Arqueología Hondureña,
       Copan, Honduras.
Willey, Gordon R.
 1945 Horizon Styles and Pottery Traditions in Peruvian Archaeology.
       American Antiquity 11:49–56.
 1972 *The Artifacts of Altar de Sacrificios.* Harvard University Peabody
       Museum of Archaeology and Ethnology Papers 64 (1). Cambridge,
       Mass.
 1973 *The Altar de Sacrificios Excavations: General Summary and Con-
       clusions.* Harvard University Peabody Museum of Archaeology and
       Ethnology Papers 64 (3). Cambridge, Mass.
 1977 The Rise of Classic Maya Civilization: A Pasión Valley Perspective.
       In *The Origins of Maya Civilization*, edited by Richard E. W. Adams,
       pp. 133–158. Albuquerque: University of New Mexico Press.
 1978 *Excavations at Seibal: Artifacts.* Harvard University Peabody Mu-
       seum of Archaeology and Ethnology Memoirs 14. Cambridge, Mass.
 1981 Maya Lowland Settlement Patterns: A Summary Review. In *Low-
       land Maya Settlement Patterns*, edited by Wendy Ashmore, pp.
       385–415. Albuquerque: University of New Mexico Press.
 1986 The Classic Maya Sociopolitical Order: A Study in Coherence and
       Instability. In *Research and Reflections in Archaeology and His-
       tory: Essays in Honor of Doris Stone*, edited by E. W. Andrews,
       pp. 189–198. Tulane University, Middle American Research Insti-
       tute Publication 57. New Orleans.

Willey, Gordon R., William Bullard, James Gifford, and John Glass
 1965 *Prehistoric Maya Settlements in the Belize Valley.* Harvard University Peabody Museum of Archaeology and Ethnology Papers 54. Cambridge, Mass.
Willey, Gordon R., and Philip Phillips
 1958 *Method and Theory in American Archaeology.* Chicago: University of Chicago Press.
Willey, Gordon R., and Jeremy A. Sabloff
 1974 *A History of American Archaeology.* San Francisco: W. H. Freeman and Co.
Williams, Howel, and A. R. McBirney
 1969 *Volcanic History of Honduras.* University of California Publications in Geological Sciences 85. Berkeley: University of California Press.
Wisdom, Charles
 1940 *The Chorti Indians of Guatemala.* Chicago: University of Chicago Press.
Wobst, H. M.
 1977 Stylistic Behavior and Information Theory. In *Papers for the Director: Research Essays in Honor of James B. Griffin,* edited by Charles Edward Cleland, pp. 317–342. Anthropological Papers of the Museum of Anthropology of the University of Michigan, no. 61. Ann Arbor.
Wonderley, Anthony
 1981 *Late Postclassic Excavations at Naco, Honduras.* Latin American Studies Program, Dissertation Series 86. Ithaca: Cornell University.
 1984a The Land of Ulua at Conquest. In *Archaeology in Northwestern Honduras: Interim Reports of the Proyecto Arqueologico Sula,* vol. 1, edited by John S. Henderson, pp. 4–26. Ithaca: Archaeology Program–Latin American Studies Program, Cornell University.
 1984b Rancho Ires Phase (Colonial) Test Excavations. In *Archaeology in Northwestern Honduras: Interim Reports of the Proyecto Arqueologico Sula,* vol. 1, edited by John S. Henderson, pp. 67–79. Ithaca: Archaeology Program–Latin American Studies Program, Cornell University.
 1984c Test Excavations of the Naco (Late Postclassic) Phase. In *Archaeology in Northwestern Honduras: Interim Reports of the Proyecto Arqueológico Sula,* vol. 1, edited by John S. Henderson, pp. 27–66. Ithaca: Archaeology Program–Latin American Studies Program, Cornell University.
 1985 The Land of Ulua: Postclassic Research in the Naco and Sula Valleys, Honduras. In *The Lowland Maya Postclassic,* edited by Arlen F. Chase and Prudence M. Rice, pp. 254–269. Austin: University of Texas Press.
 1986a Material Symbolics in Pre-Columbian Households: The Painted Pottery of Naco, Honduras. *Journal of Anthropological Research* 42(4):497–534.

1986b Naco, Honduras—Some Aspects of a Late Precolumbian Community on the Eastern Maya Frontier. In *The Southeast Maya Periphery*, edited by Patricia A. Urban and Edward M. Schortman, pp. 313–332. Austin: University of Texas Press.

1987   Imagery in Household Pottery from "La Gran Provincia de Naco." In *Interaction on the Southeast Mesoamerican Frontier: Prehistoric and Historic Honduras and El Salvador*, edited by Eugenia J. Robinson. BAR International Series 327(ii): 304–327. Oxford.

1988   The Late Preclassic Uapala Ceramic Sphere on the Eastern Edge of Mesoamerica: A View from the Sula Plain, Honduras. Presented in the symposium "Reconstructing Behavior and Social Organization: New Interpretations from Southeast Mesoamerica," Annual Meeting of the Society for American Archaeology, Phoenix.

Wonderley, Anthony, and Pauline Caputi

1983   Archaeological Investigations at Rio Pelo (YR 125). A report submitted to the Proyecto Arqueológico Sula, Instituto Hondureño de Antropología e Historia, Tegucigalpa.

Author Index

Subject Index